This Book Reading Diary Belongs To

_____

_____

_____

My Book List

#	Book titles

My Book List

#	Book titles

My Book List

#	Book titles

Book Review

Title

_____

Author

_____

Number of pages

_____

Draw the main character

Book Review

Describe main character

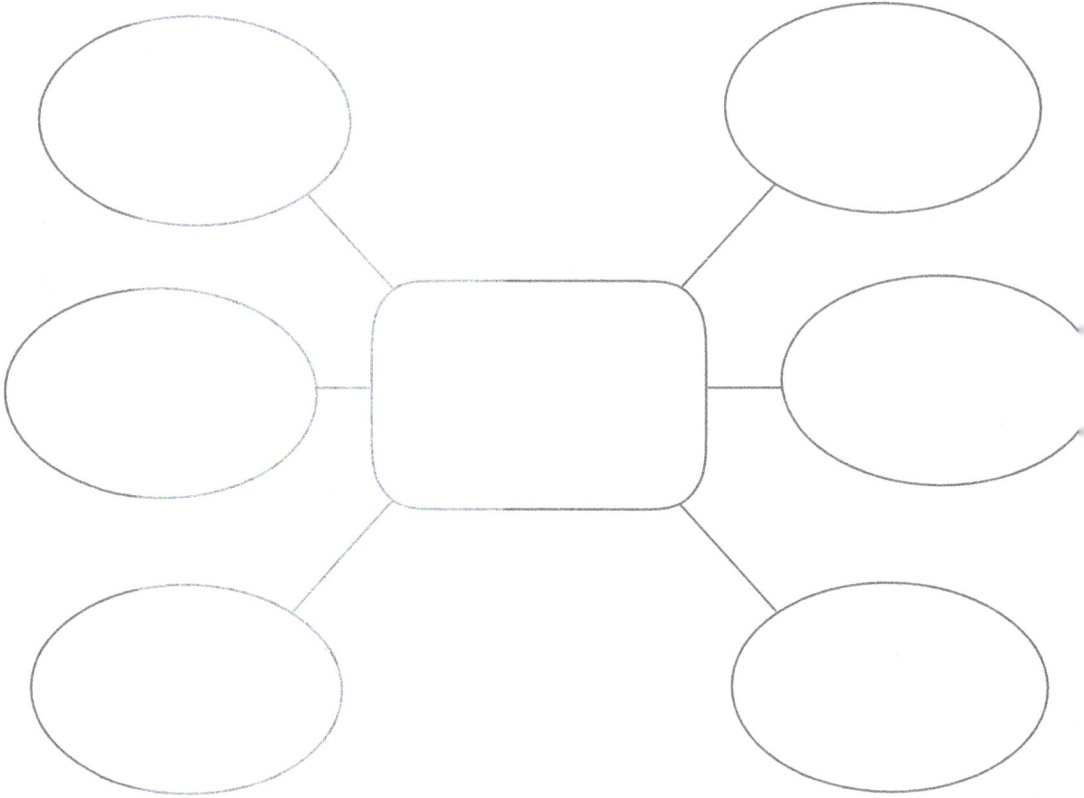

Did You like this book? Color the little sun, which most reflected your mood when reading this book

I like it !

I don't know

I don't like it

What this book is about

_____

_____

_____

_____

_____

_____

_____

What is the main event of this book   What did You learn from this book

_____   _____

_____   _____

_____   _____

_____   _____

_____   _____

_____   _____

Book Review

Title

Author

Number of pages

Draw the main character

Book Review

Describe main character

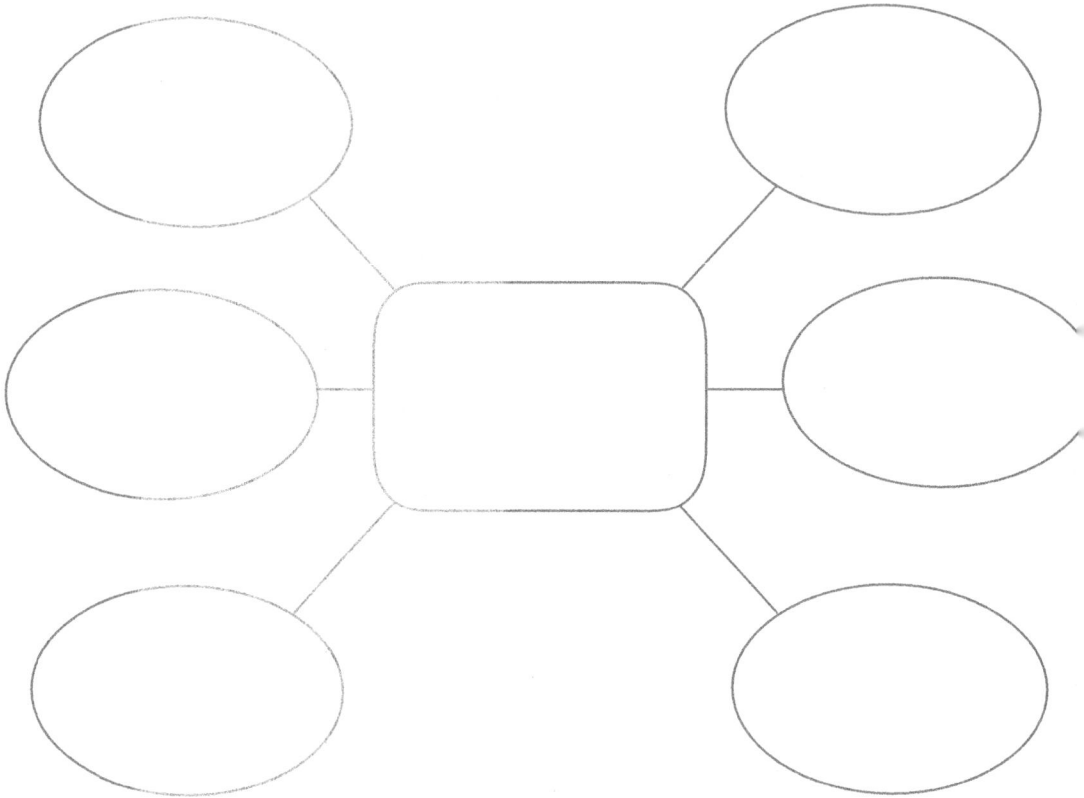

Did You like this book? Color the little sun, which most reflected your mood when reading this book

I like it !

I don't know

I don't like it

What this book is about

_____

_____

_____

_____

_____

_____

What is the main event of this book

What did You learn from this book

_____   _____

_____   _____

_____   _____

_____   _____

_____   _____

_____   _____

Book Review

Title

Author

Number of pages

Draw the main character

Book Review

Describe main character

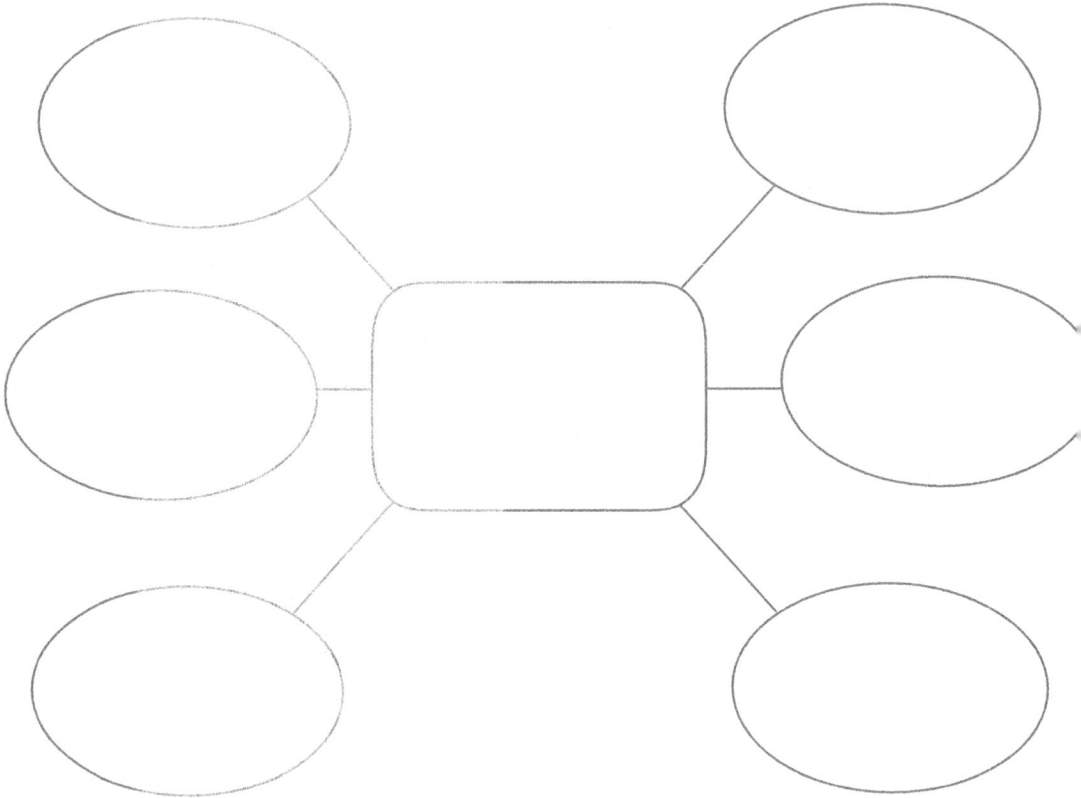

(central concept map with one rectangle in the center connected to six empty ovals)

_____

_____

_____

_____

_____

_____

_____

_____

Did You like this book? Color the little sun, which most reflected your mood when reading this book

I like it !

I don't know

I don't like it

What this book is about

_____

_____

_____

_____

_____

_____

_____

What is the main event of this book

_____

_____

_____

_____

_____

What did You learn from this book

_____

_____

_____

_____

_____

Book Review

Title

Author

Number of pages

Draw the main character

Book Review

Describe main character

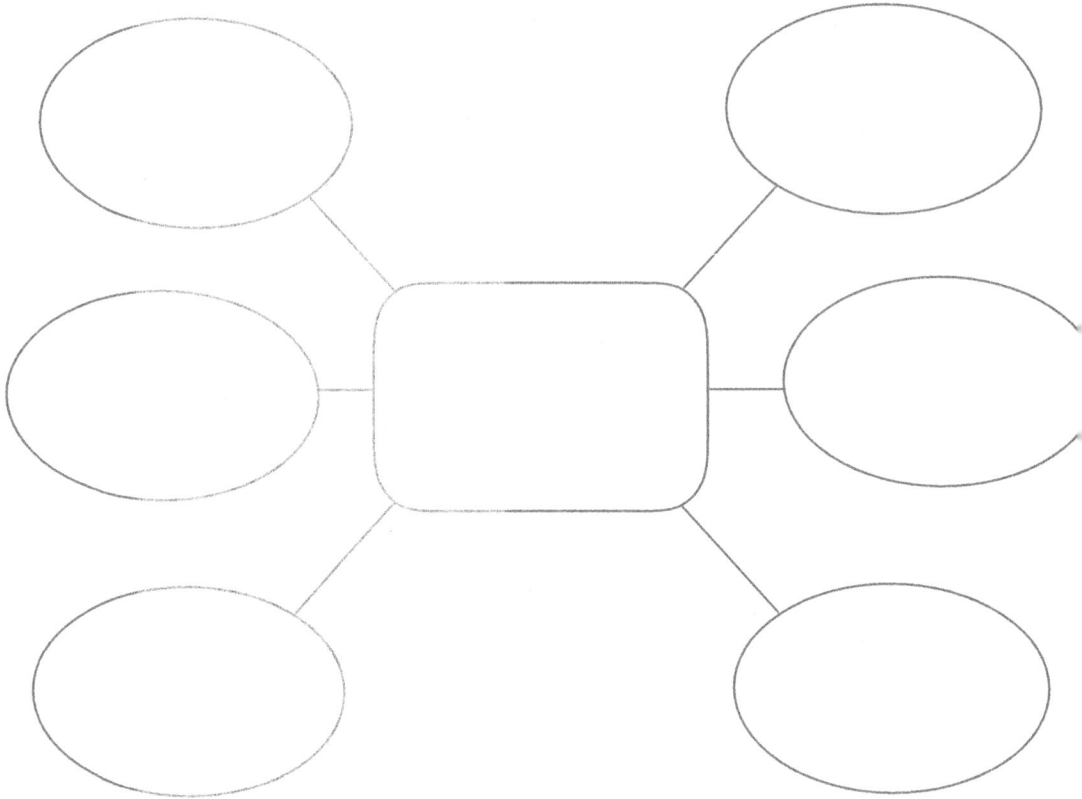

Did You like this book? Color the little sun, which most reflected your mood when reading this book

I like it !

I don't know

I don't like it

What this book is about

_____

_____

_____

_____

_____

_____

What is the main event of this book   What did You learn from this book

_____   _____

_____   _____

_____   _____

_____   _____

_____   _____

Book Review

Title

Author

Number of pages

Draw the main character

Book Review

Describe main character

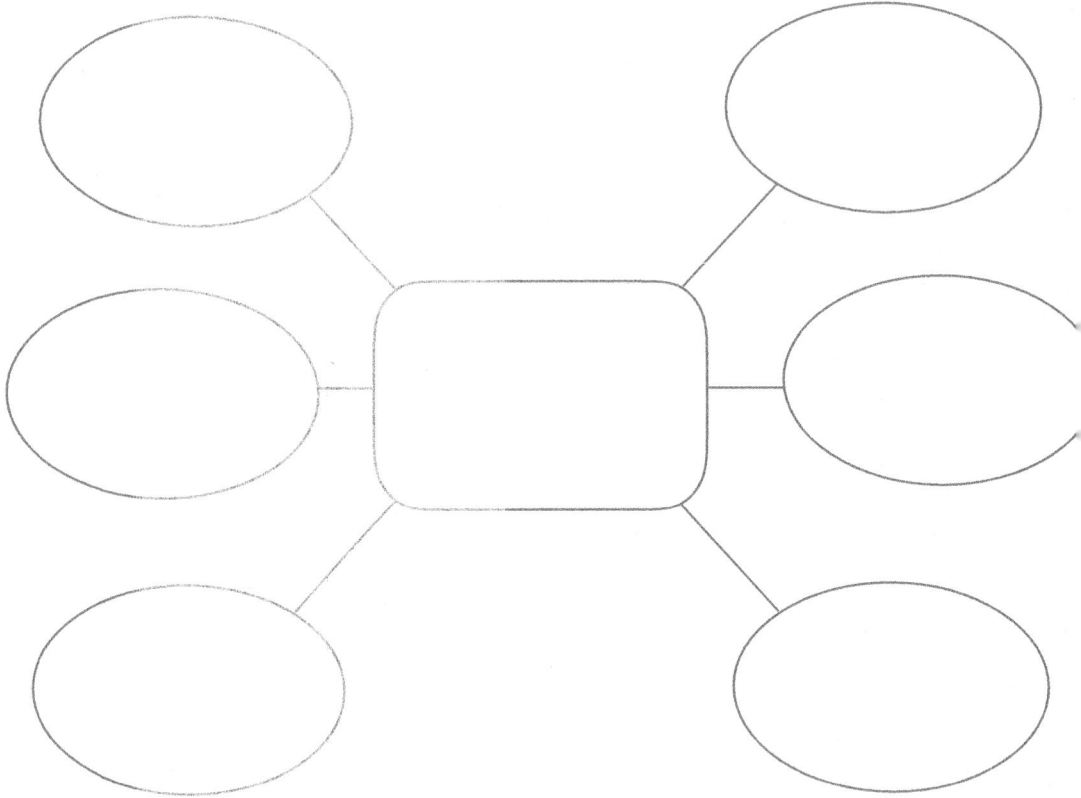

Did You like this book? Color the little sun, which most reflected your mood when reading this book

I like it !

I don't know

I don't like it

What this book is about

_____

_____

_____

_____

_____

_____

_____

What is the main event of this book   What did You learn from this book

Book Review

Title

_____

Author

_____

Number of pages

_____

Draw the main character

Book Review

Describe main character

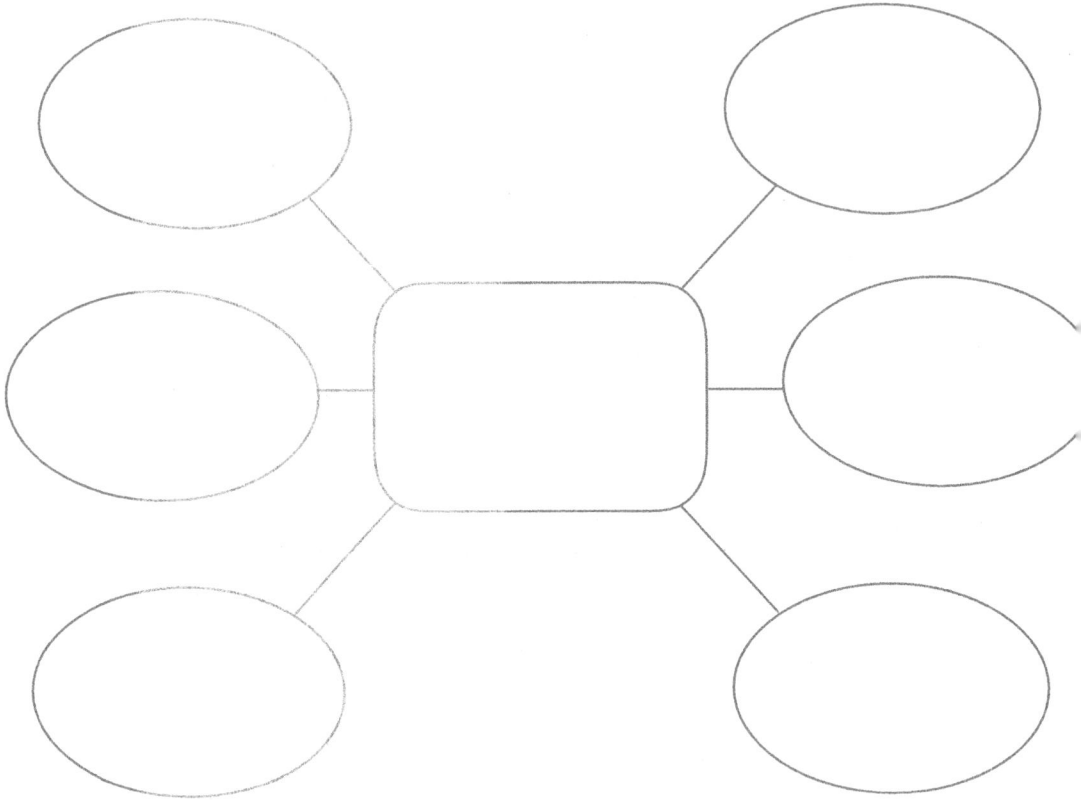

Did You like this book? Color the little sun, which most reflected your mood when reading this book

I like it !

I don't know

I don't like it

What this book is about

_____

_____

_____

_____

_____

_____

_____

What is the main event of this book   What did You learn from this book

Book Review

Title

Author

Number of pages

Draw the main character

Book Review

Describe main character

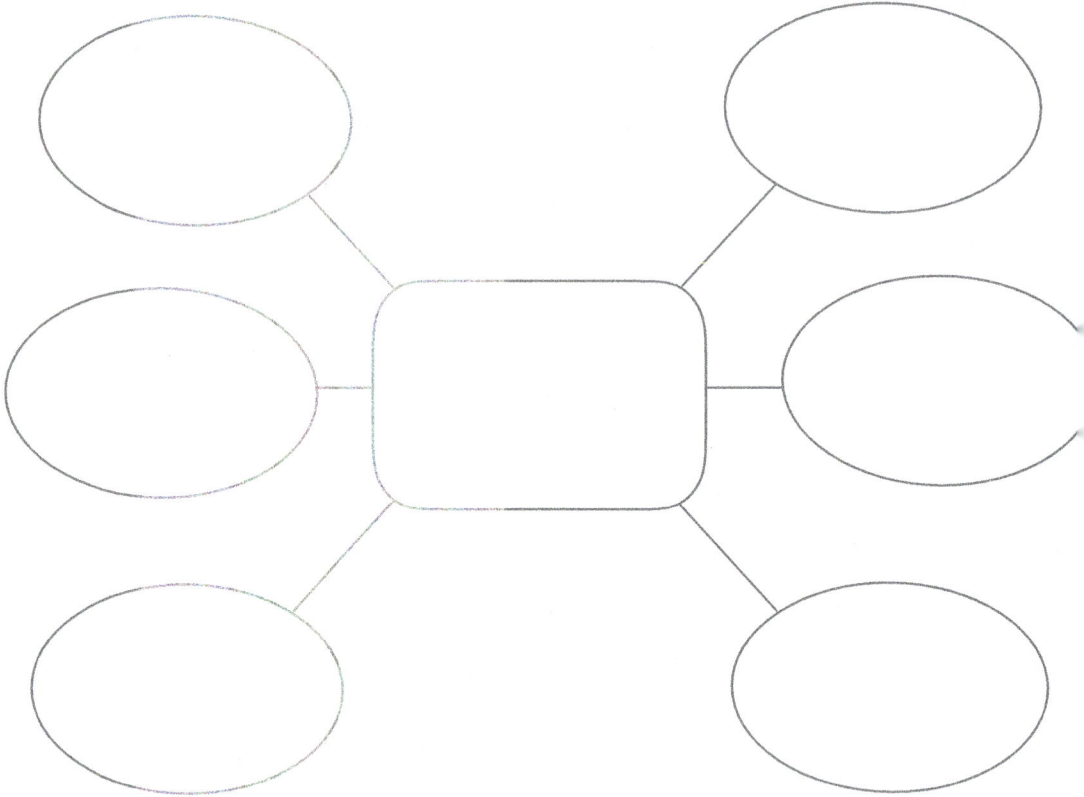

Did You like this book? Color the little sun, which most reflected your mood when reading this book

I like it !

I don't know

I don't like it

What this book is about

_____

_____

_____

_____

_____

_____

What is the main event of this book   What did You learn from this book

_____   _____

_____   _____

_____   _____

_____   _____

_____   _____

Book Review

Title

_____

Author

_____

Number of pages

_____

Draw the main character

Book Review

Describe main character

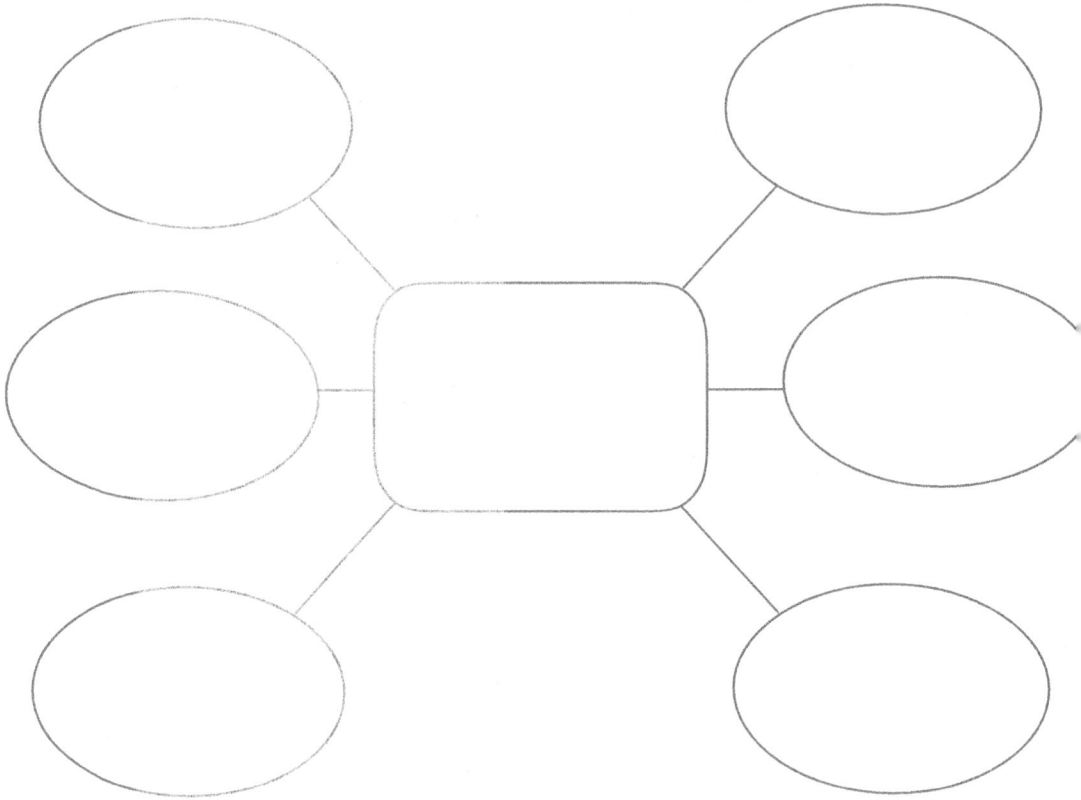

_____
_____
_____
_____
_____
_____
_____

Did You like this book? Color the little sun, which most reflected your mood when reading this book

I like it !

I don't know

I don't like it

What this book is about

_____

_____

_____

_____

_____

_____

_____

What is the main event of this book   What did You learn from this book

_____   _____

_____   _____

_____   _____

_____   _____

_____   _____

Book Review

Title

Author

Number of pages

Draw the main character

Book Review

Describe main character

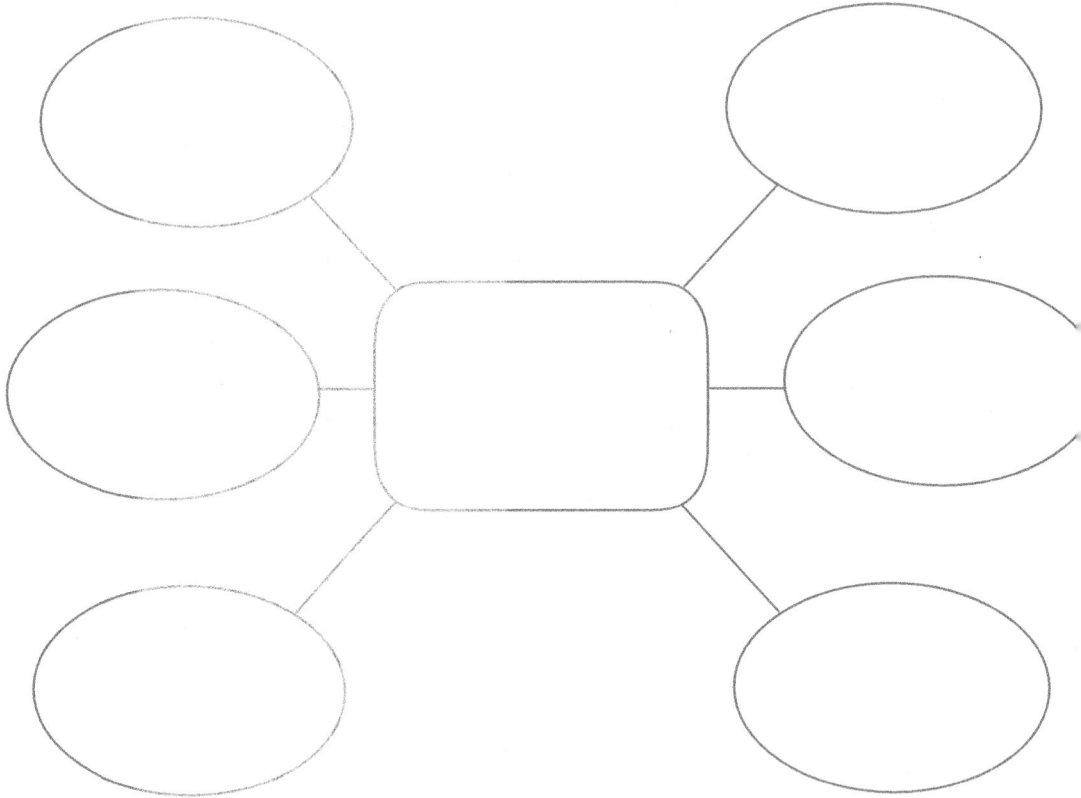

Did You like this book? Color the little sun, which most reflected your mood when reading this book

I like it !

I don't know

I don't like it

What this book is about

_____

_____

_____

_____

_____

_____

What is the main event of this book   What did You learn from this book

Book Review

Title

Author

Number of pages

Draw the main character

Book Review

Describe main character

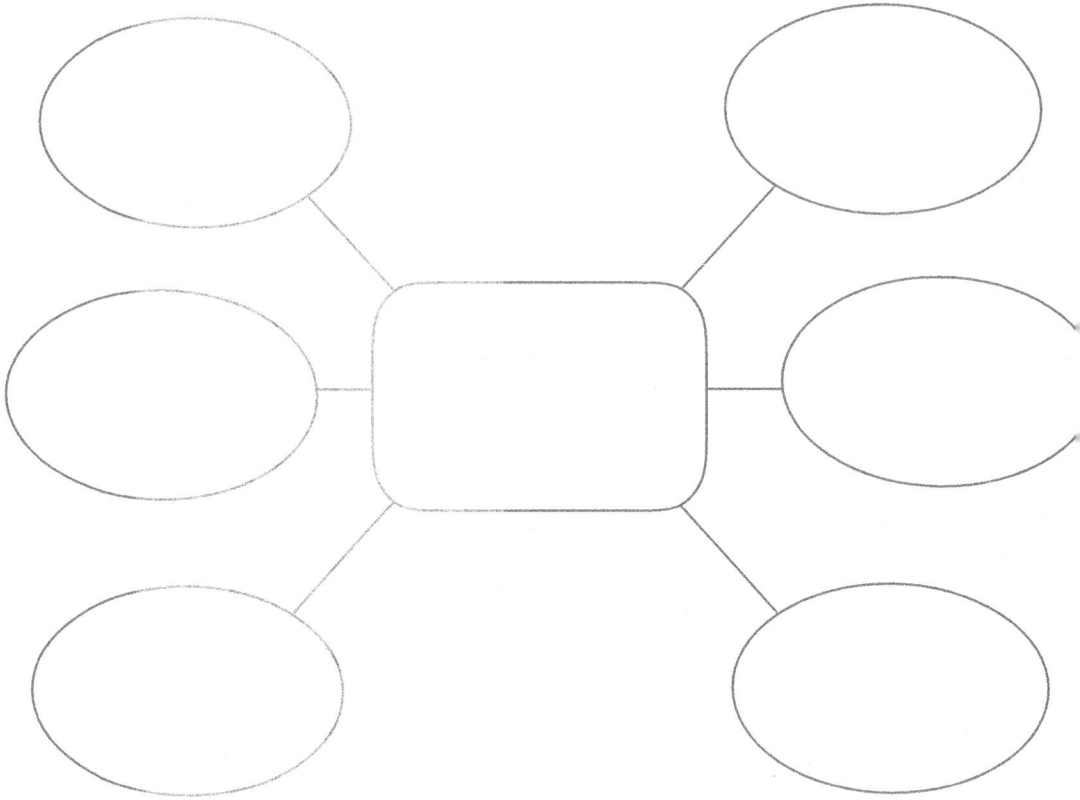

Did You like this book? Color the little sun, which most reflected your mood when reading this book

I like it !

I don't know

I don't like it

What this book is about

_____

_____

_____

_____

_____

_____

What is the main event of this book   What did You learn from this book

_____   _____

_____   _____

_____   _____

_____   _____

_____   _____

_____   _____

Book Review

Title

Author

Number of pages

Draw the main character

Book Review

Describe main character

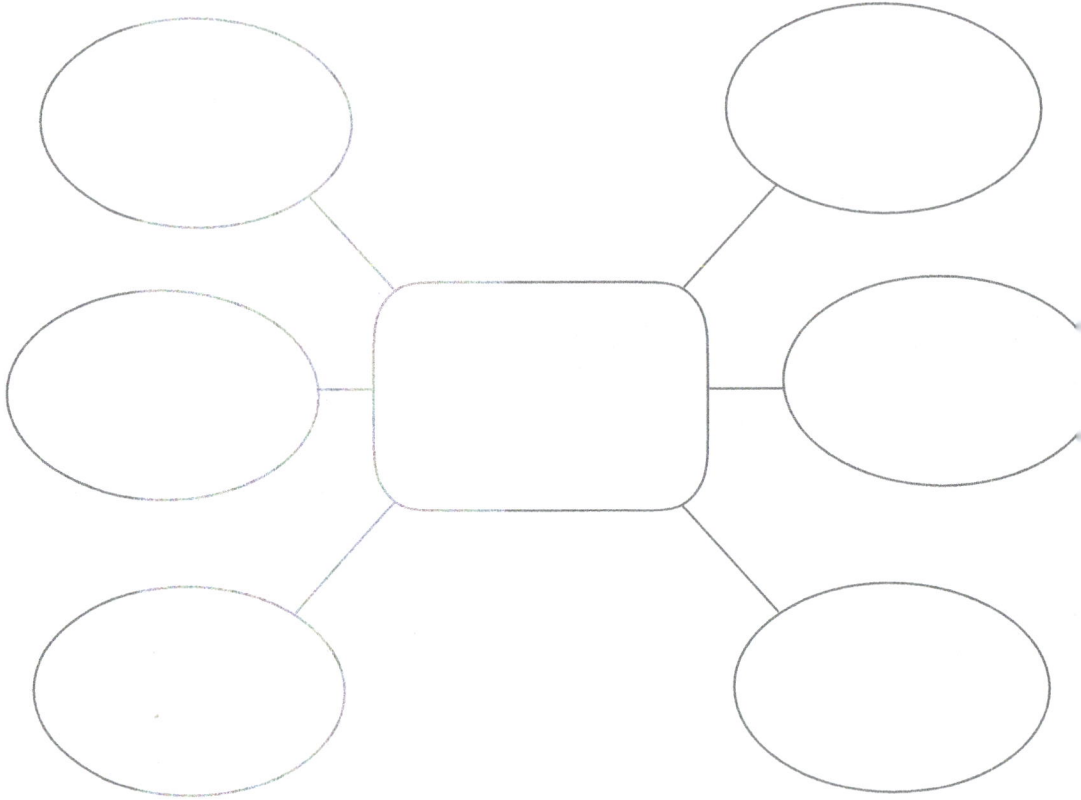

_____
_____
_____
_____
_____
_____
_____
_____

Did You like this book? Color the little sun, which most reflected your mood when reading this book

I like it !

I don't know

I don't like it

What this book is about

_____

_____

_____

_____

_____

_____

_____

What is the main event of this book   What did You learn from this book

_____   _____

_____   _____

_____   _____

_____   _____

_____   _____

Book Review

Title

Author

Number of pages

Draw the main character

Book Review

Describe main character

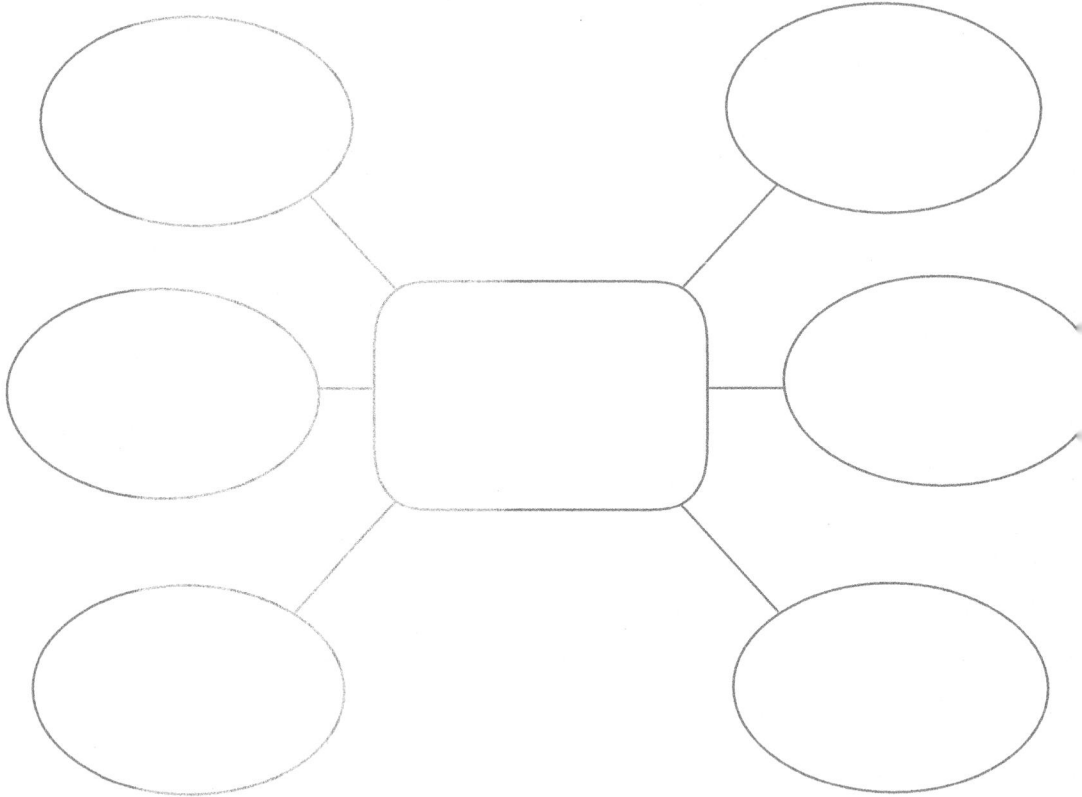

Did You like this book? Color the little sun, which most reflected your mood when reading this book

I like it !

I don't know

I don't like it

What this book is about

_____

_____

_____

_____

_____

_____

_____

What is the main event of this book   What did You learn from this book

Book Review

Title

Author

Number of pages

Draw the main character

Book Review

Describe main character

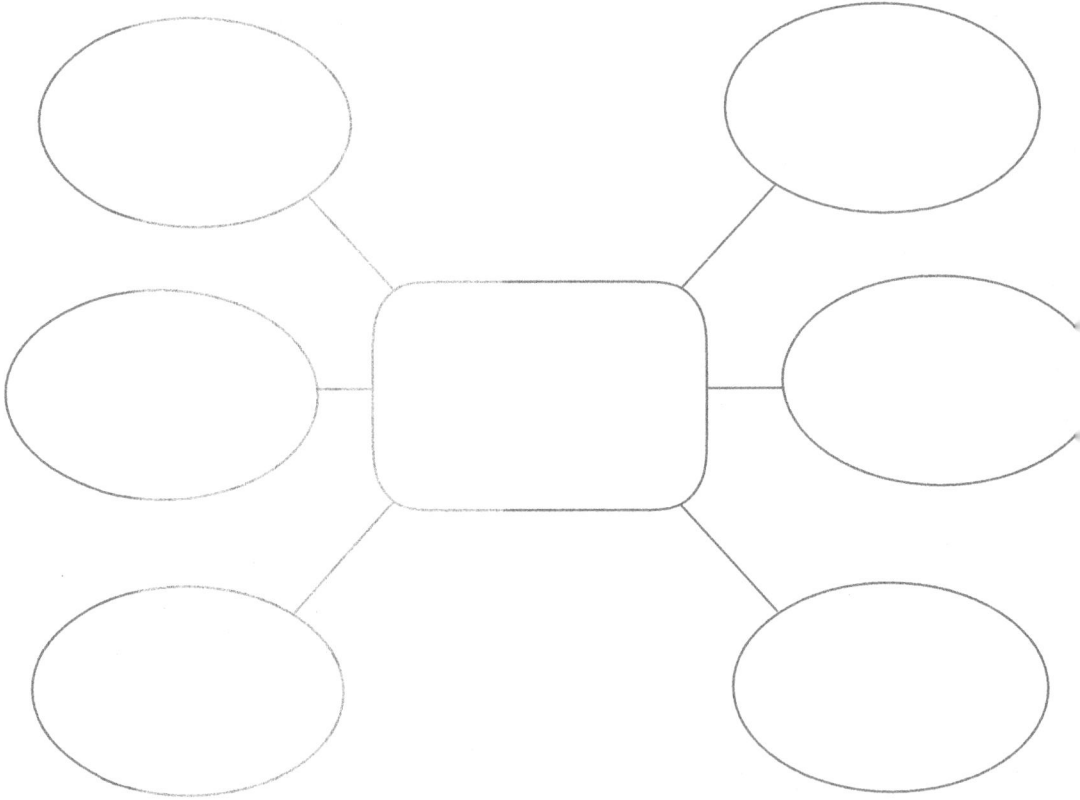

Did You like this book? Color the little sun, which most reflected your mood when reading this book

I like it !

I don't know

I don't like it

What this book is about

_____

_____

_____

_____

_____

_____

What is the main event of this book   What did You learn from this book

Book Review

Title

Author

Number of pages

Draw the main character

Book Review

Describe main character

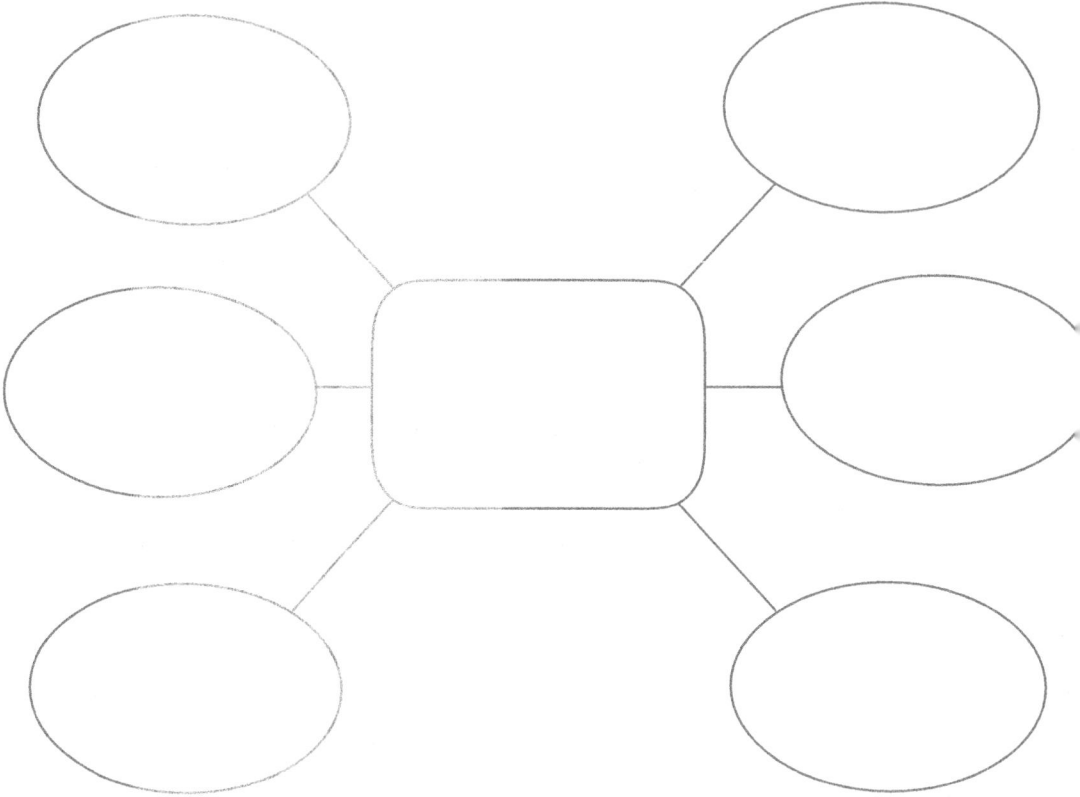

(graphic organizer: central rounded rectangle connected to six surrounding ovals)

_____
_____
_____
_____
_____
_____
_____
_____

Did You like this book? Color the little sun, which most reflected your mood when reading this book

I like it !

I don't know

I don't like it

What this book is about

_____

_____

_____

_____

_____

_____

What is the main event of this book   What did You learn from this book

Book Review

Title

Author

Number of pages

Draw the main character

Book Review

Describe main character

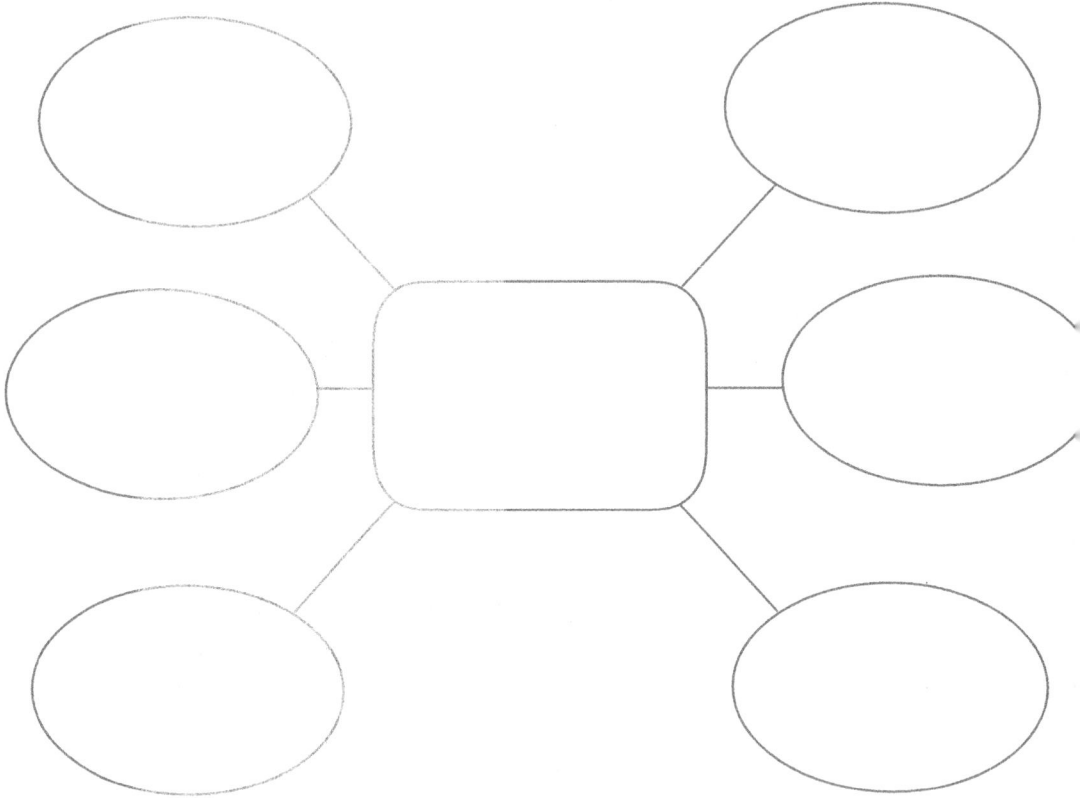

Did You like this book? Color the little sun, which most reflected your mood when reading this book

I like it !

I don't know

I don't like it

What this book is about

_____

_____

_____

_____

_____

_____

_____

What is the main event of this book   What did You learn from this book

_____   _____

_____   _____

_____   _____

_____   _____

_____   _____

_____   _____

Book Review

Title

Author

Number of pages

Draw the main character

Book Review

Describe main character

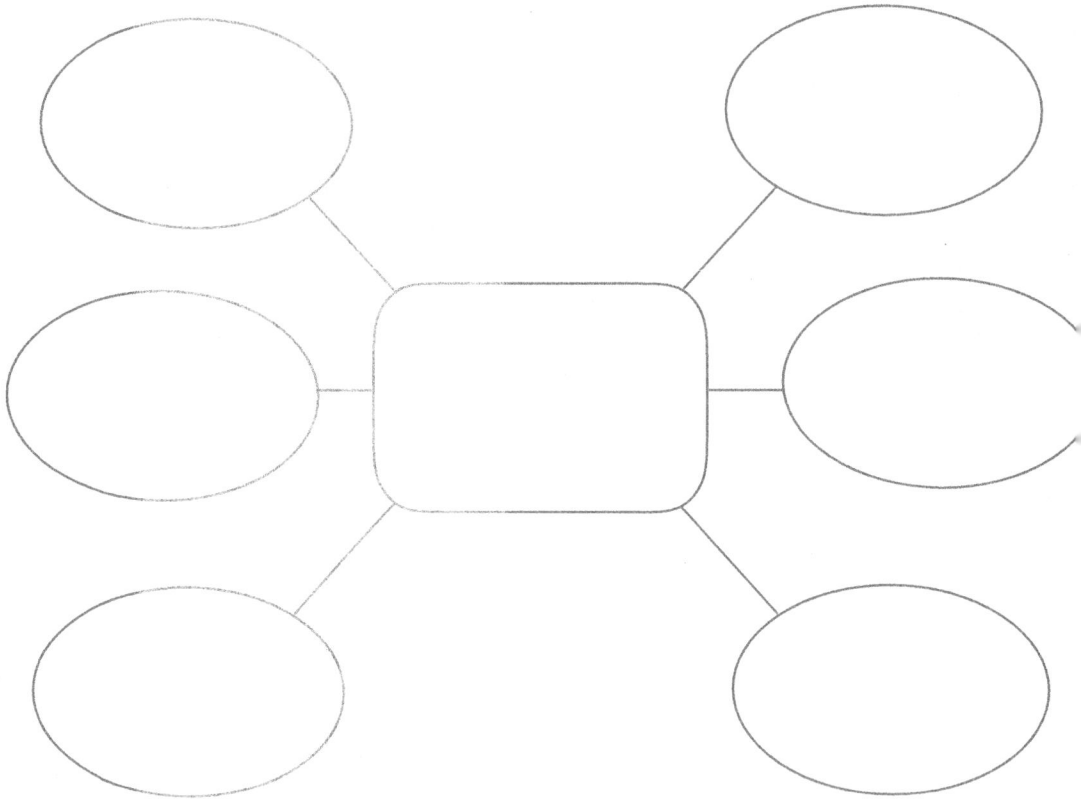

_____

_____

_____

_____

_____

_____

_____

_____

Did You like this book? Color the little sun, which most reflected your mood when reading this book

I like it !

I don't know

I don't like it

What this book is about

_____

_____

_____

_____

_____

_____

_____

What is the main event of this book   What did You learn from this book

_____   _____

_____   _____

_____   _____

_____   _____

_____   _____

Book Review

Title

Author

Number of pages

Draw the main character

Book Review

Describe main character

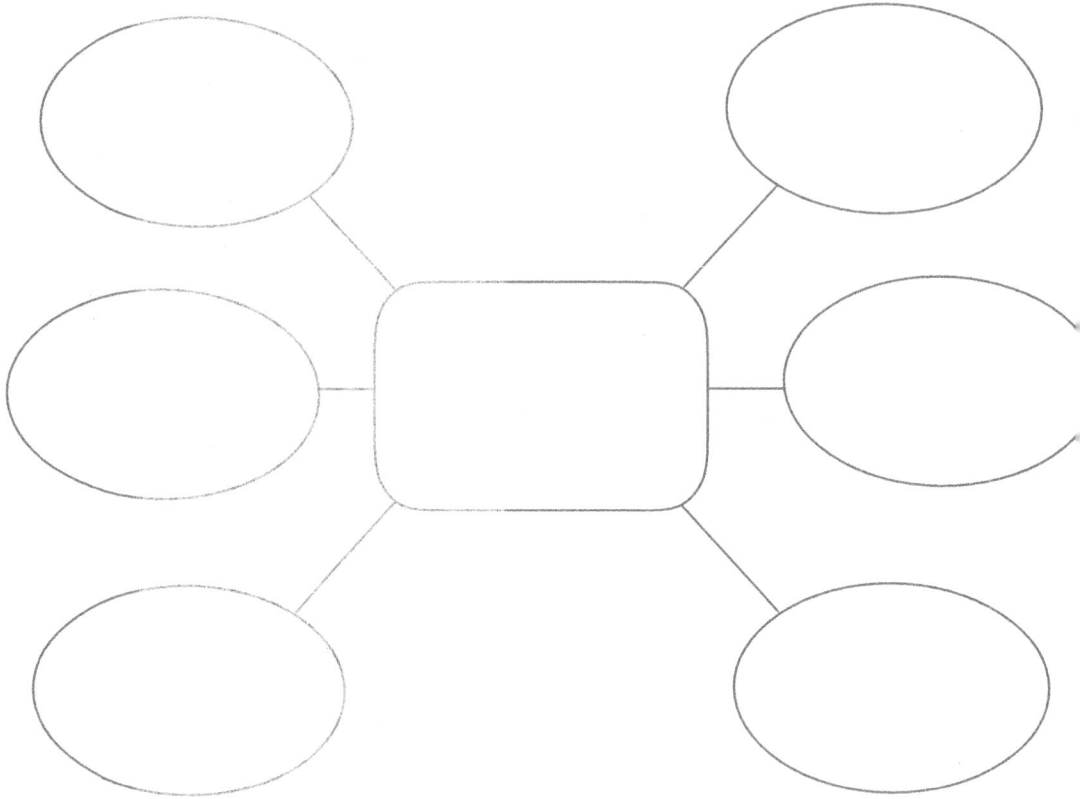

Did You like this book? Color the little sun, which most reflected your mood when reading this book

I like it !

I don't know

I don't like it

What this book is about

_____

_____

_____

_____

_____

_____

_____

What is the main event of this book   What did You learn from this book

Book Review

Title

_____

Author

_____

Number of pages

_____

Draw the main character

Book Review

Describe main character

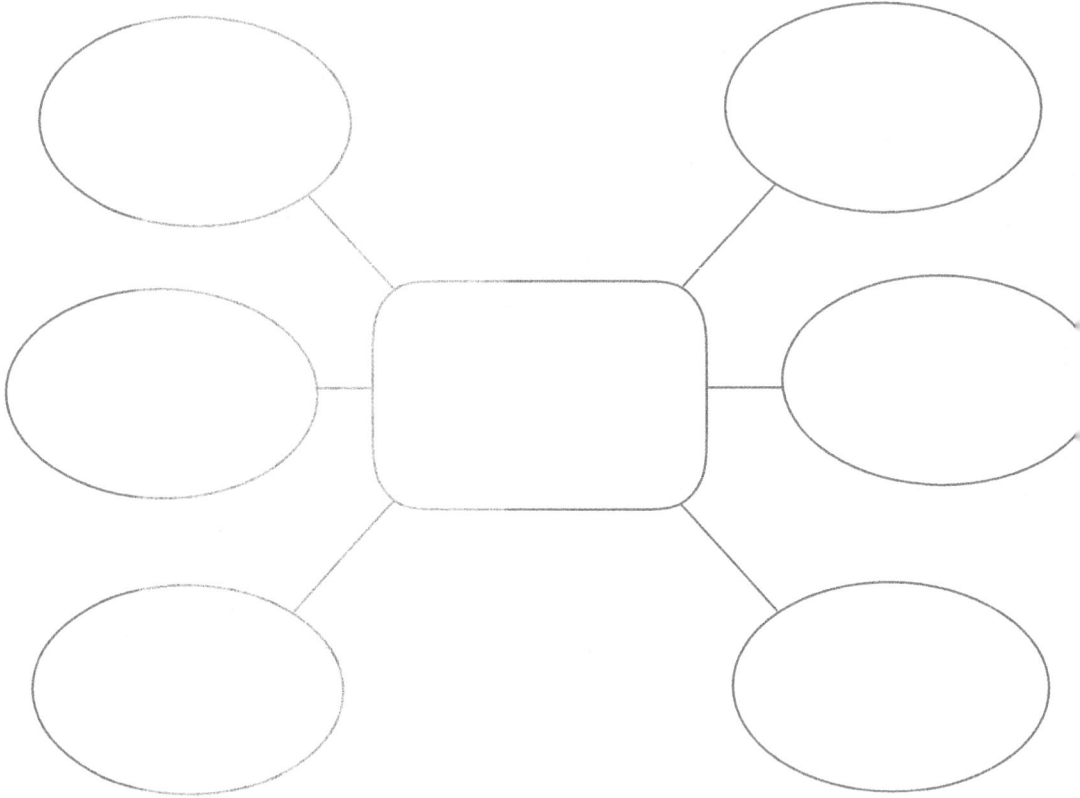

Did You like this book? Color the little sun, which most reflected your mood when reading this book

I like it !

I don't know

I don't like it

What this book is about

_____

_____

_____

_____

_____

_____

What is the main event of this book   What did You learn from this book

_____   _____

_____   _____

_____   _____

_____   _____

_____   _____

Book Review

Title

Author

Number of pages

Draw the main character

Book Review

Describe main character

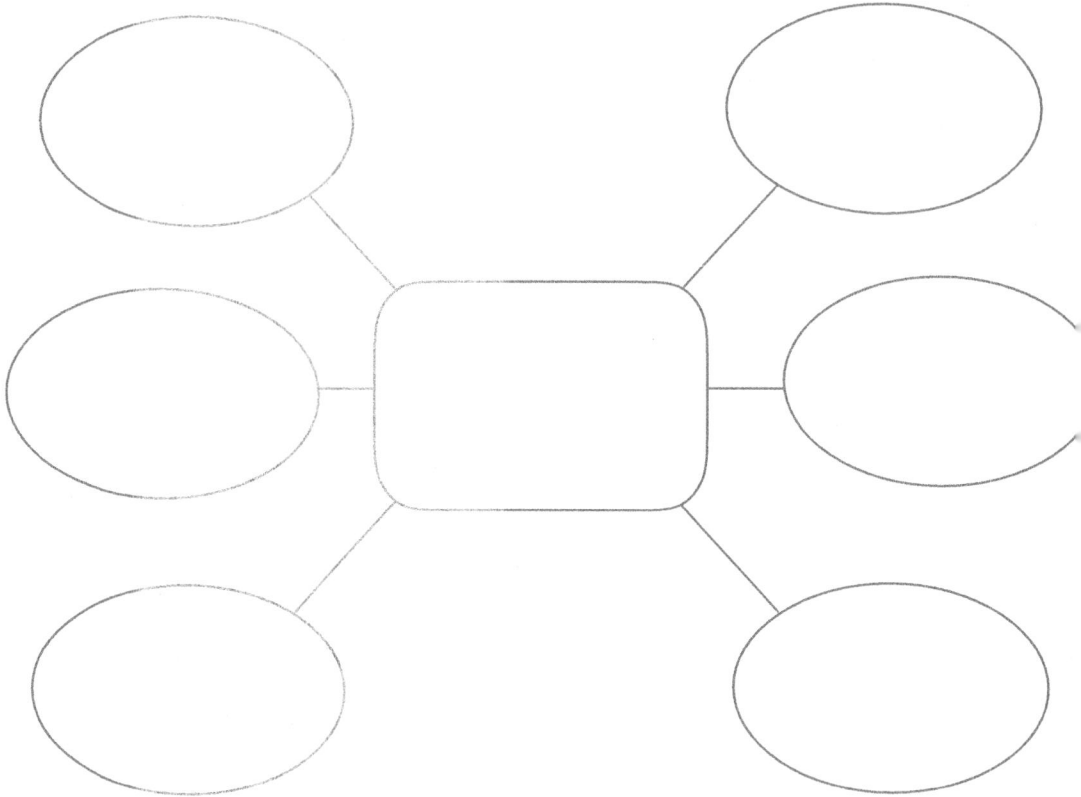

Did You like this book? Color the little sun, which most reflected your mood when reading this book

I like it !

I don't know

I don't like it

What this book is about

_____

_____

_____

_____

_____

_____

_____

What is the main event of this book

_____

_____

_____

_____

_____

What did You learn from this book

_____

_____

_____

_____

_____

Book Review

Title

Author

Number of pages

Draw the main character

Book Review

Describe main character

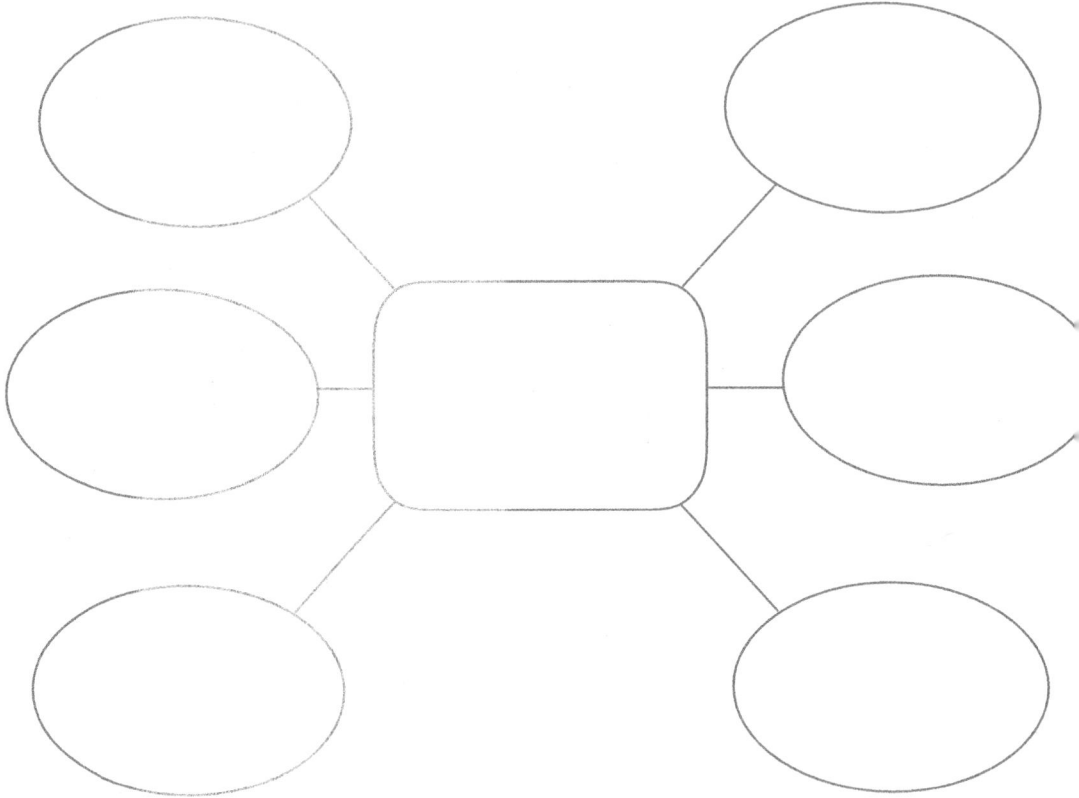

Did You like this book? Color the little sun, which most reflected your mood when reading this book

I like it !   I don't know   I don't like it

What this book is about

_____

_____

_____

_____

_____

_____

_____

What is the main event of this book   What did You learn from this book

Book Review

Title

Author

Number of pages

Draw the main character

Book Review

Describe main character

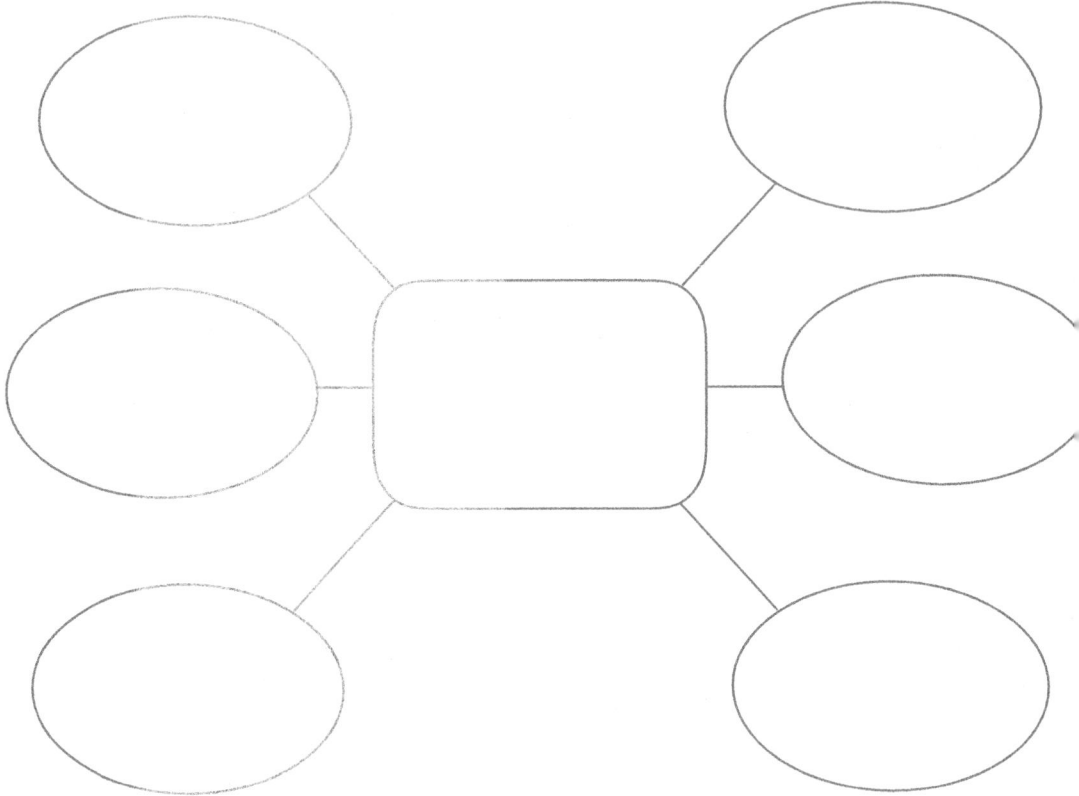

Did You like this book? Color the little sun, which most reflected your
mood when reading this book

I like it !

I don't know

I don't like it

- - - What this book is about - - -

_____

_____

_____

_____

_____

_____

_____

What is the main event of this book   What did You learn from this book

_____   _____

_____   _____

_____   _____

_____   _____

_____   _____

Book Review

Title

_____

Author

_____

Number of pages

_____

Draw the main character

Book Review

Describe main character

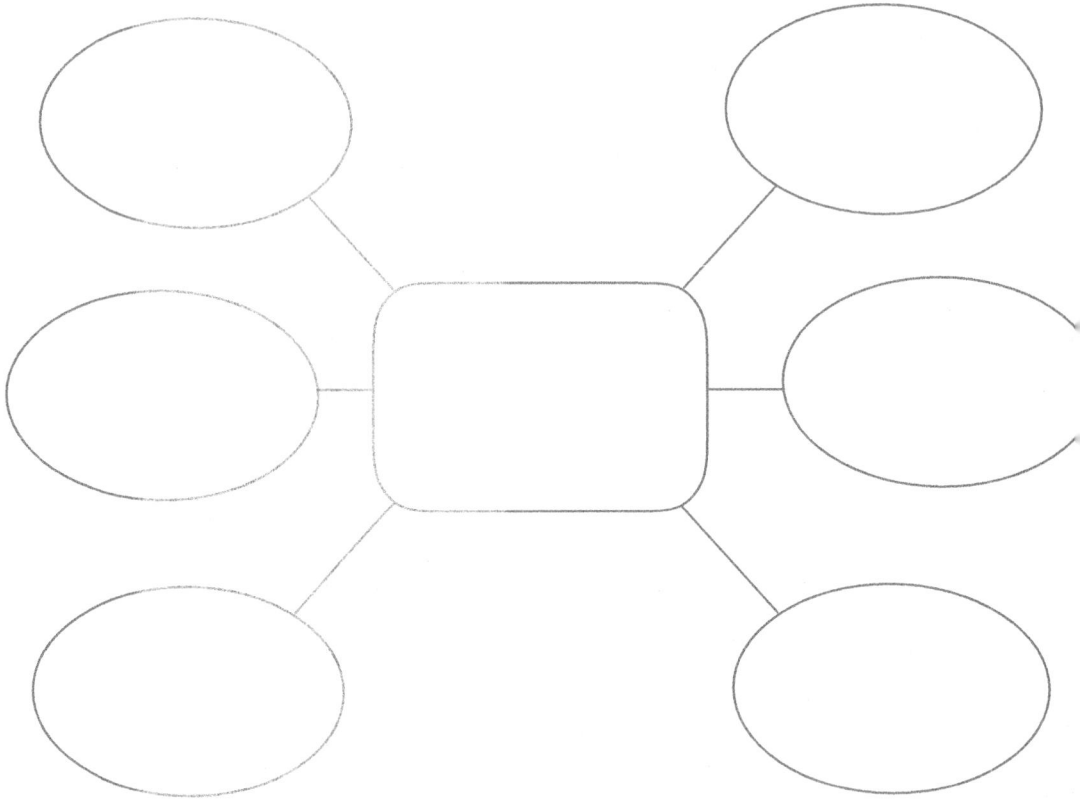

_____
_____
_____
_____
_____
_____
_____

Did You like this book? Color the little sun, which most reflected your mood when reading this book

I like it !

I don't know

I don't like it

What this book is about

_____

_____

_____

_____

_____

_____

What is the main event of this book   What did You learn from this book

_____   _____

_____   _____

_____   _____

_____   _____

_____   _____

Book Review

Title

Author

Number of pages

Draw the main character

Book Review

Describe main character

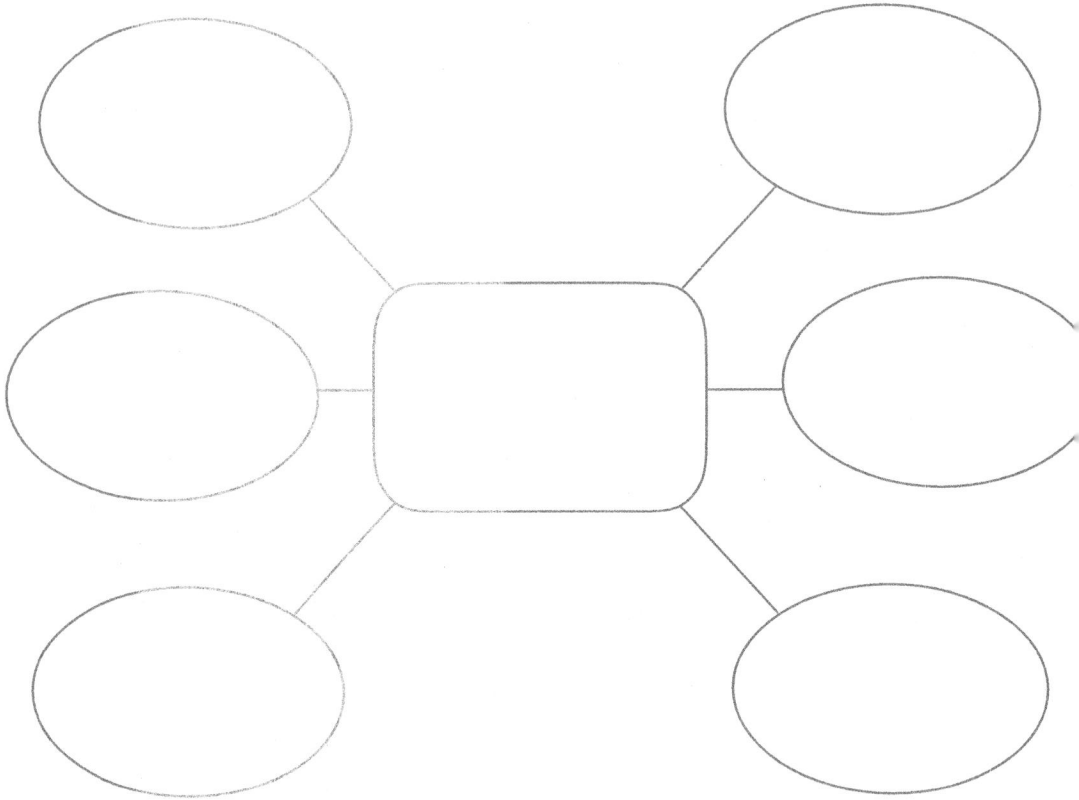

Did You like this book? Color the little sun, which most reflected your mood when reading this book

I like it !

I don't know

I don't like it

----What this book is about ----

_____

_____

_____

_____

_____

_____

What is the main event of this book   What did You learn from this book

_____   _____

_____   _____

_____   _____

_____   _____

_____   _____

Book Review

Title

Author

Number of pages

Draw the main character

Book Review

Describe main character

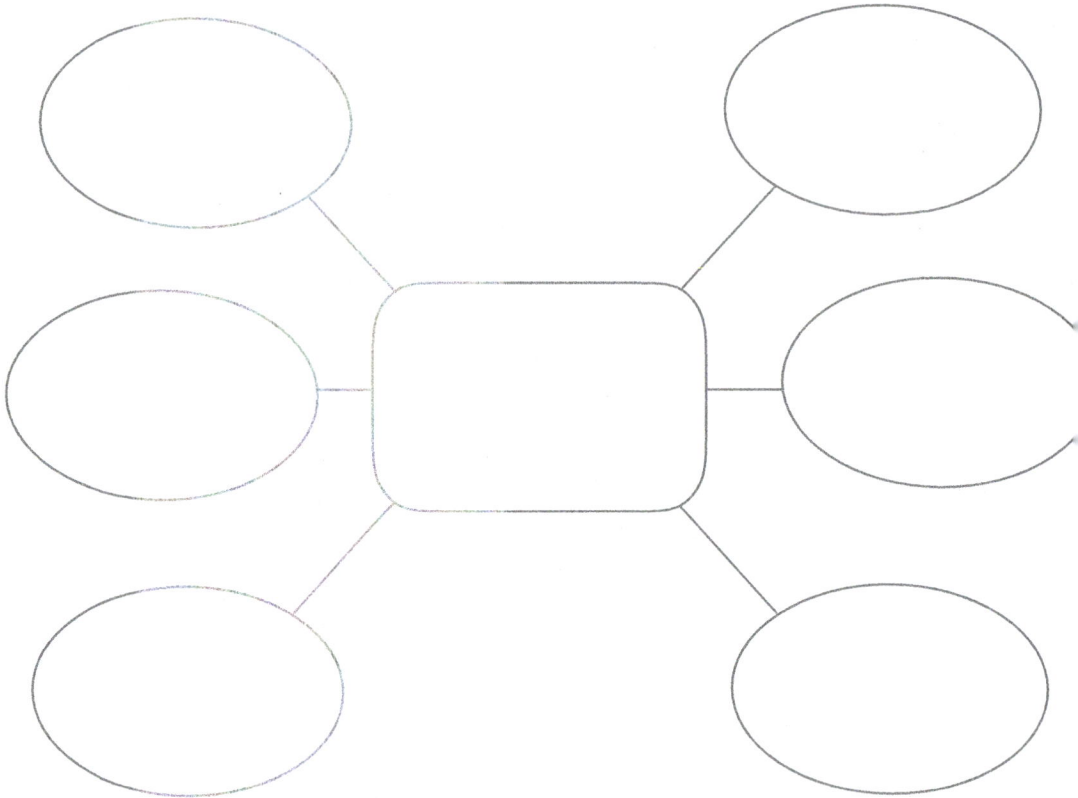

Did You like this book? Color the little sun, which most reflected your
mood when reading this book

I like it !

I don't know

I don't like it

What this book is about

_____

_____

_____

_____

_____

_____

What is the main event of this book   What did You learn from this book

_____   _____

_____   _____

_____   _____

_____   _____

_____   _____

_____   _____

Book Review

Title

Author

Number of pages

Draw the main character

Book Review

Describe main character

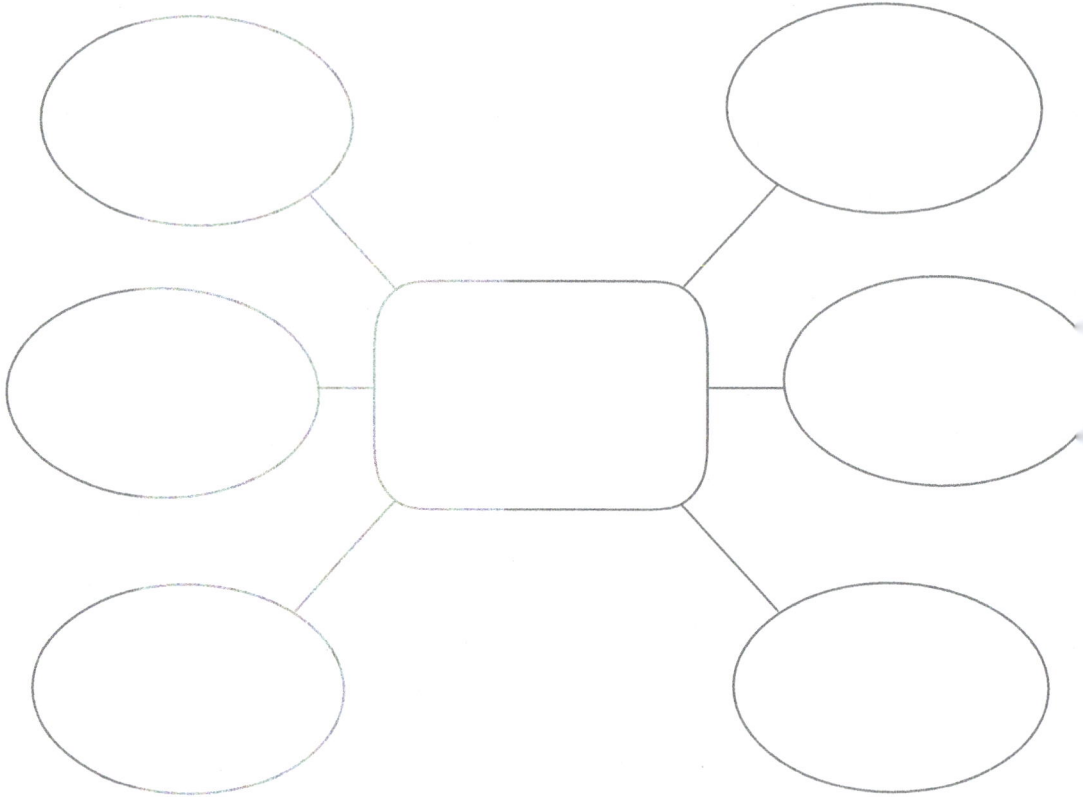

Did You like this book? Color the little sun, which most reflected your mood when reading this book

I like it !

I don't know

I don't like it

What this book is about

_____

_____

_____

_____

_____

_____

_____

What is the main event of this book   What did You learn from this book

_____   _____

_____   _____

_____   _____

_____   _____

_____   _____

Book Review

Title

Author

Number of pages

Draw the main character

Book Review

Describe main character

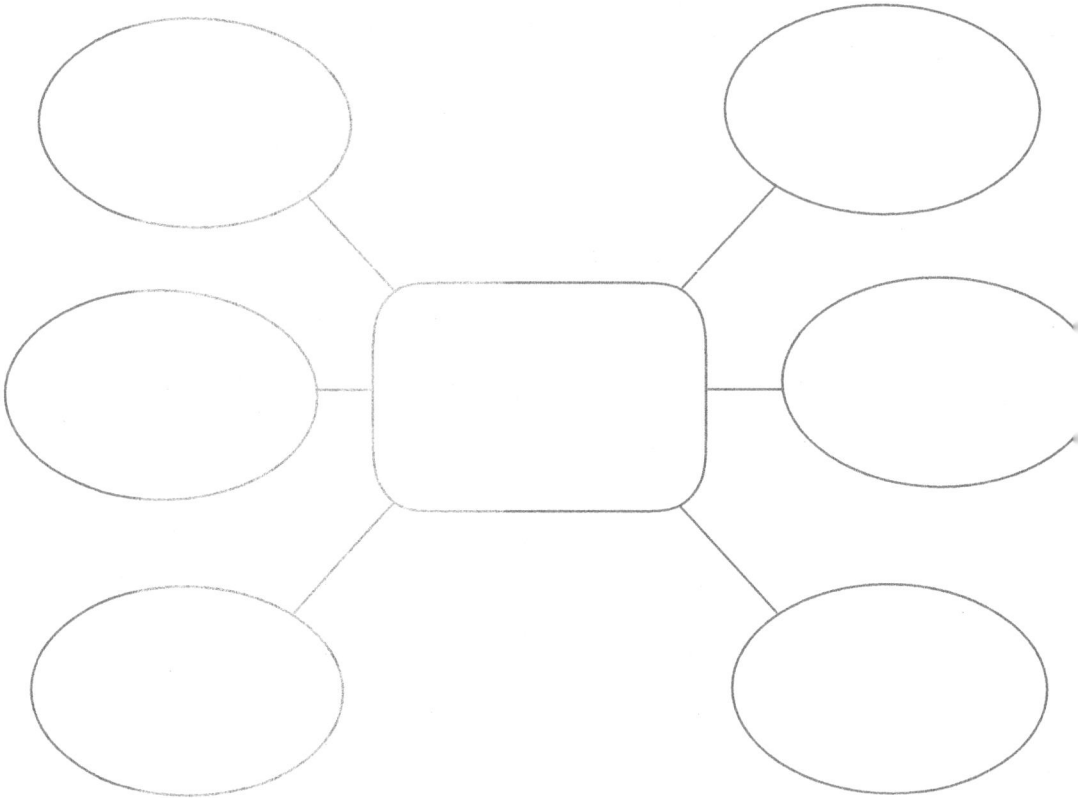

Did You like this book? Color the little sun, which most reflected your mood when reading this book

I like it !

I don't know

I don't like it

What this book is about

_____

_____

_____

_____

_____

_____

_____

What is the main event of this book   What did You learn from this book

Book Review

Title

Author

Number of pages

Draw the main character

Book Review

Describe main character

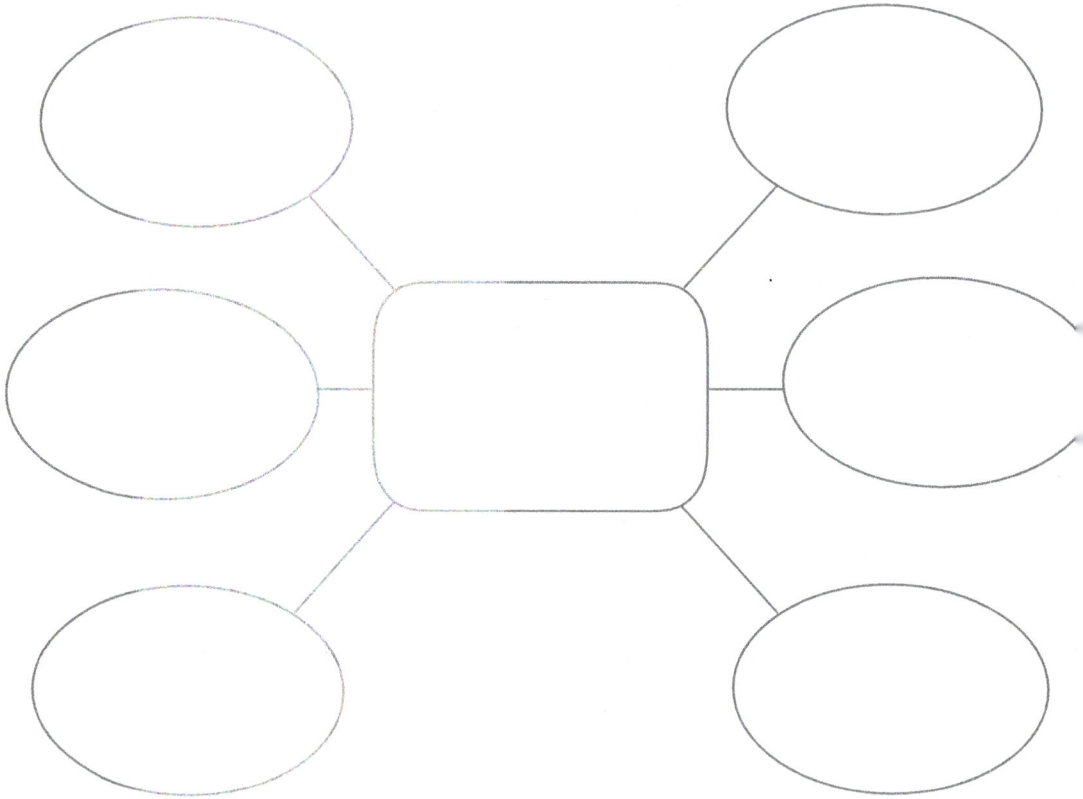

_____
_____
_____
_____
_____
_____
_____
_____

Did You like this book? Color the little sun, which most reflected your mood when reading this book

I like it !

I don't know

I don't like it

What this book is about

_____

_____

_____

_____

_____

_____

_____

What is the main event of this book   What did You learn from this book

_____   _____

_____   _____

_____   _____

_____   _____

_____   _____

_____   _____

Book Review

Title

Author

Number of pages

Draw the main character

Book Review

Describe main character

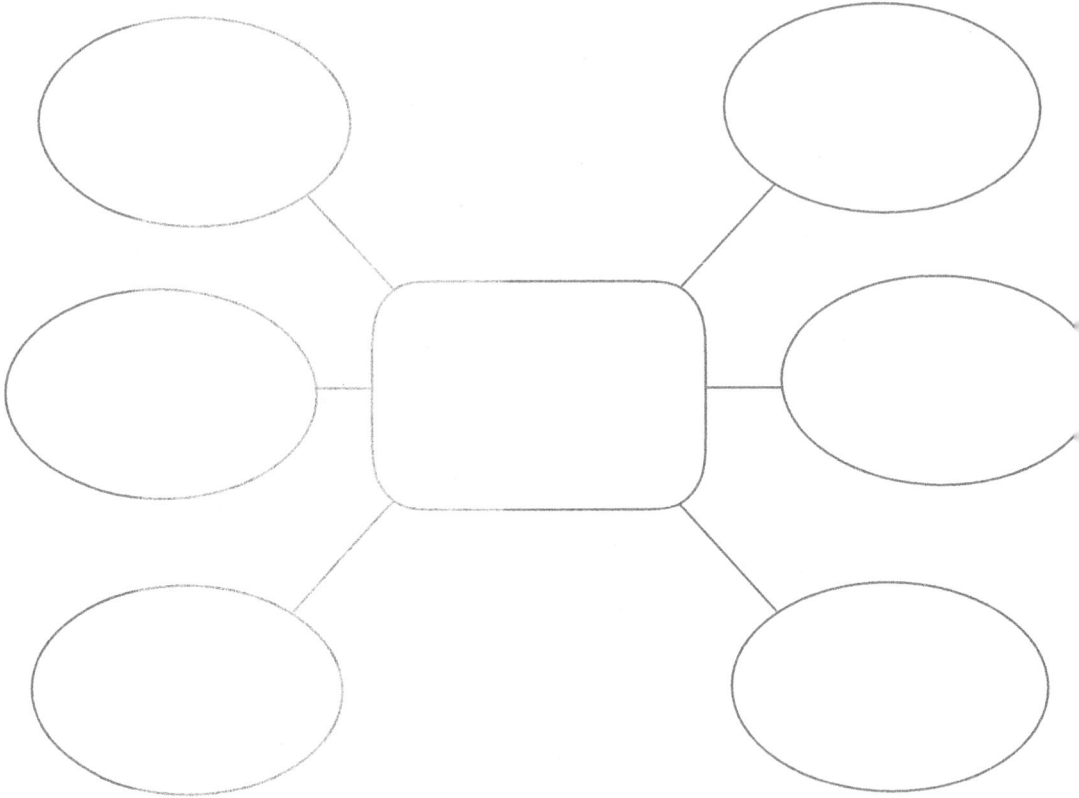

(graphic organizer: central rounded rectangle connected to six empty ovals)

_____

_____

_____

_____

_____

_____

_____

Did You like this book? Color the little sun, which most reflected your mood when reading this book

I like it !   I don't know   I don't like it

----What this book is about ----

_____

_____

_____

_____

_____

_____

What is the main event of this book   What did You learn from this book

_____   _____

_____   _____

_____   _____

_____   _____

_____   _____

Book Review

Title

Author

Number of pages

Draw the main character

Book Review

Describe main character

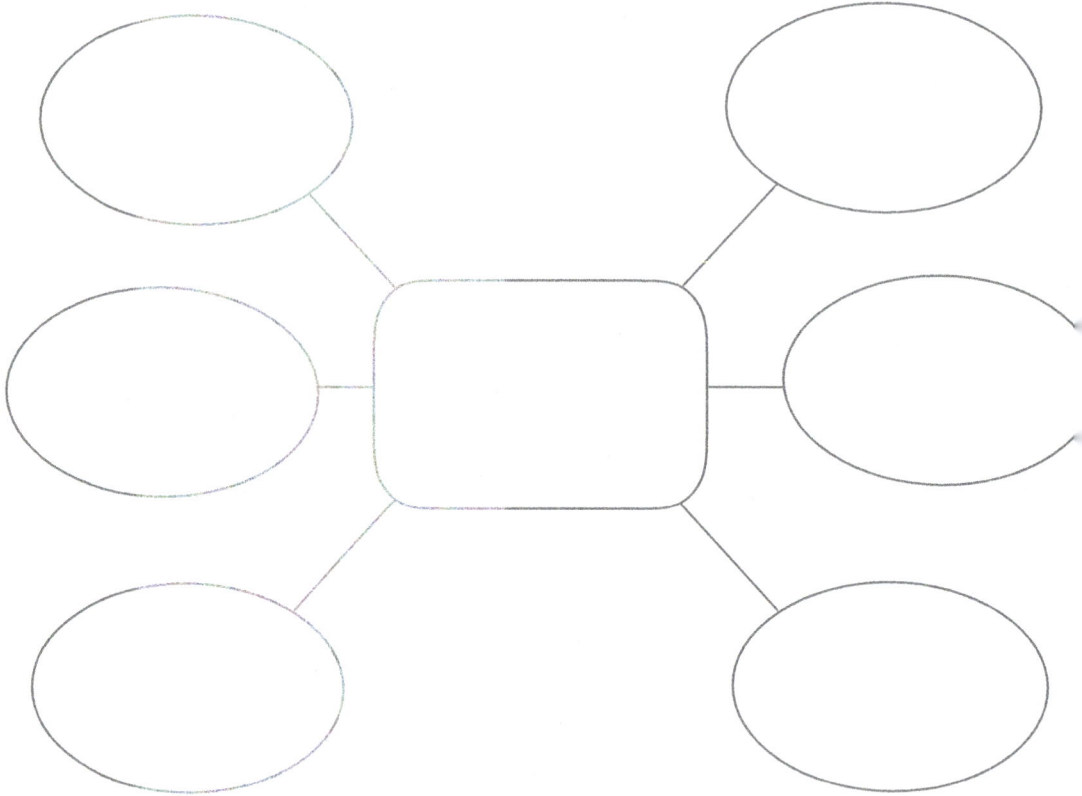

Did You like this book? Color the little sun, which most reflected your mood when reading this book

I like it !

I don't know

I don't like it

What this book is about

_____

_____

_____

_____

_____

_____

What is the main event of this book   What did You learn from this book

_____   _____

_____   _____

_____   _____

_____   _____

_____   _____

_____   _____

Book Review

Title

Author

Number of pages

Draw the main character

Book Review

Describe main character

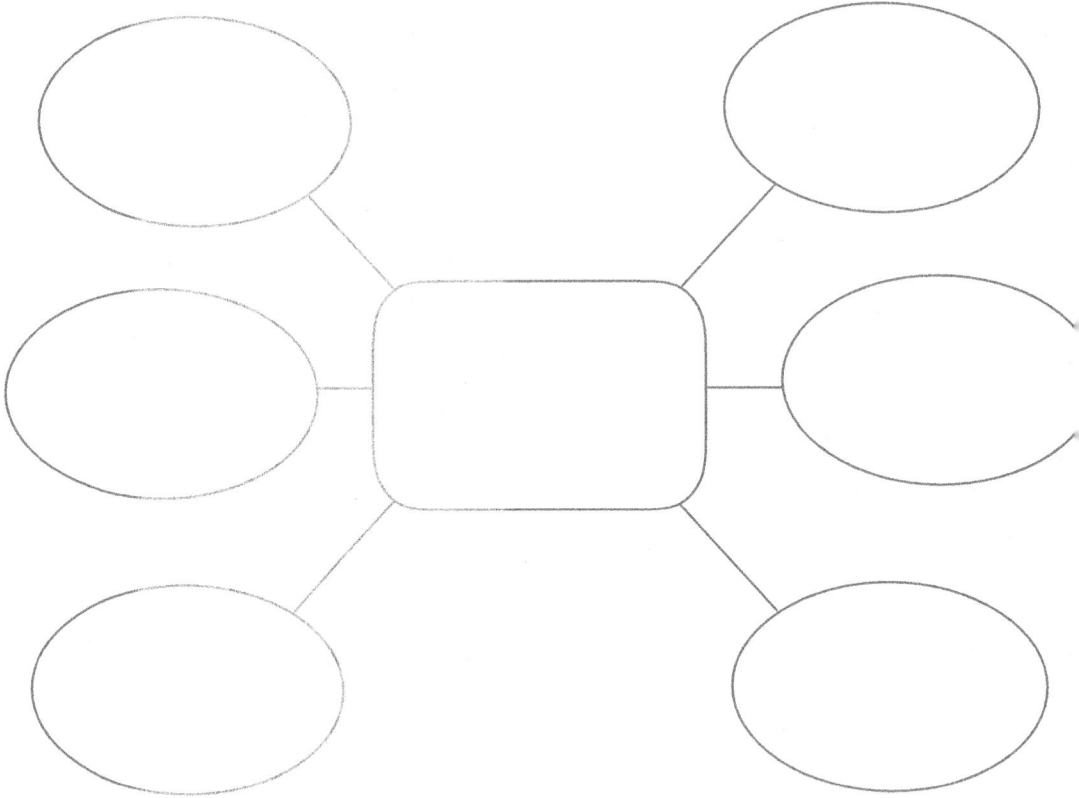

Did You like this book? Color the little sun, which most reflected your mood when reading this book

I like it !   I don't know   I don't like it

----What this book is about ----

_____

_____

_____

_____

_____

_____

What is the main event of this book   What did You learn from this book

_____   _____

_____   _____

_____   _____

_____   _____

_____   _____

_____   _____

Book Review

Title

Author

Number of pages

Draw the main character

Book Review

Describe main character

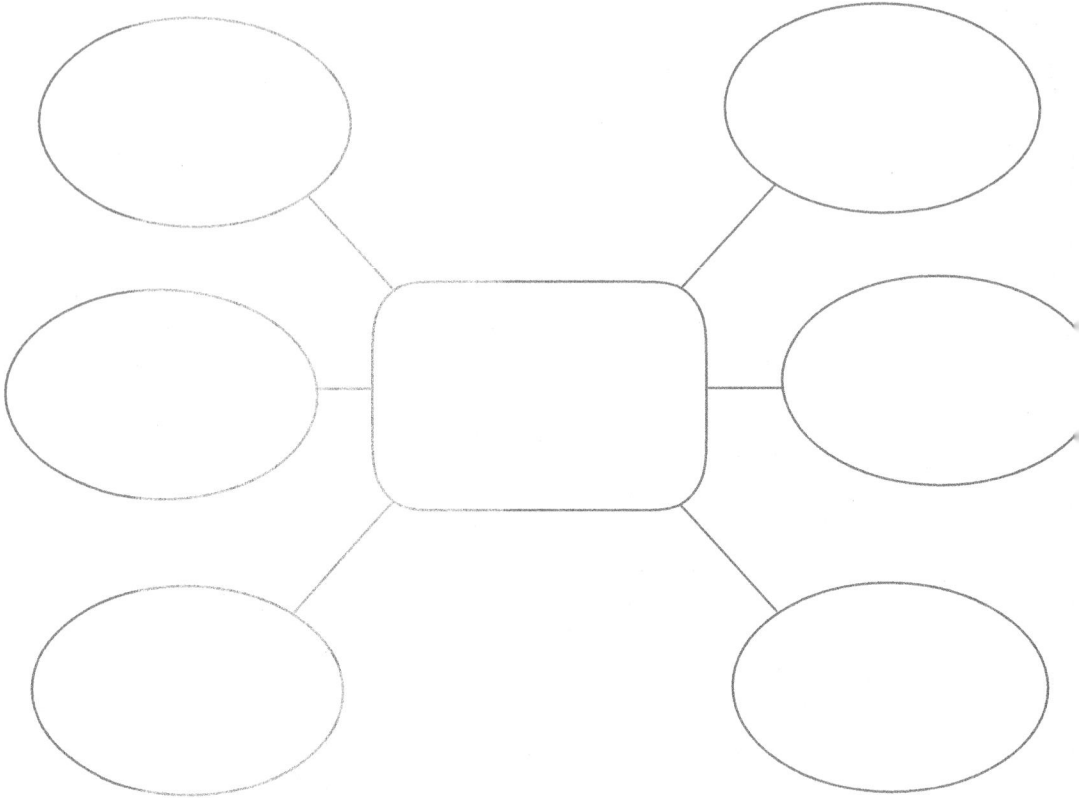

Did You like this book? Color the little sun, which most reflected your mood when reading this book

I like it !

I don't know

I don't like it

What this book is about

_____

_____

_____

_____

_____

_____

_____

What is the main event of this book   What did You learn from this book

_____   _____

_____   _____

_____   _____

_____   _____

_____   _____

Book Review

Title

_____

Author

_____

Number of pages

_____

Draw the main character

Book Review

Describe main character

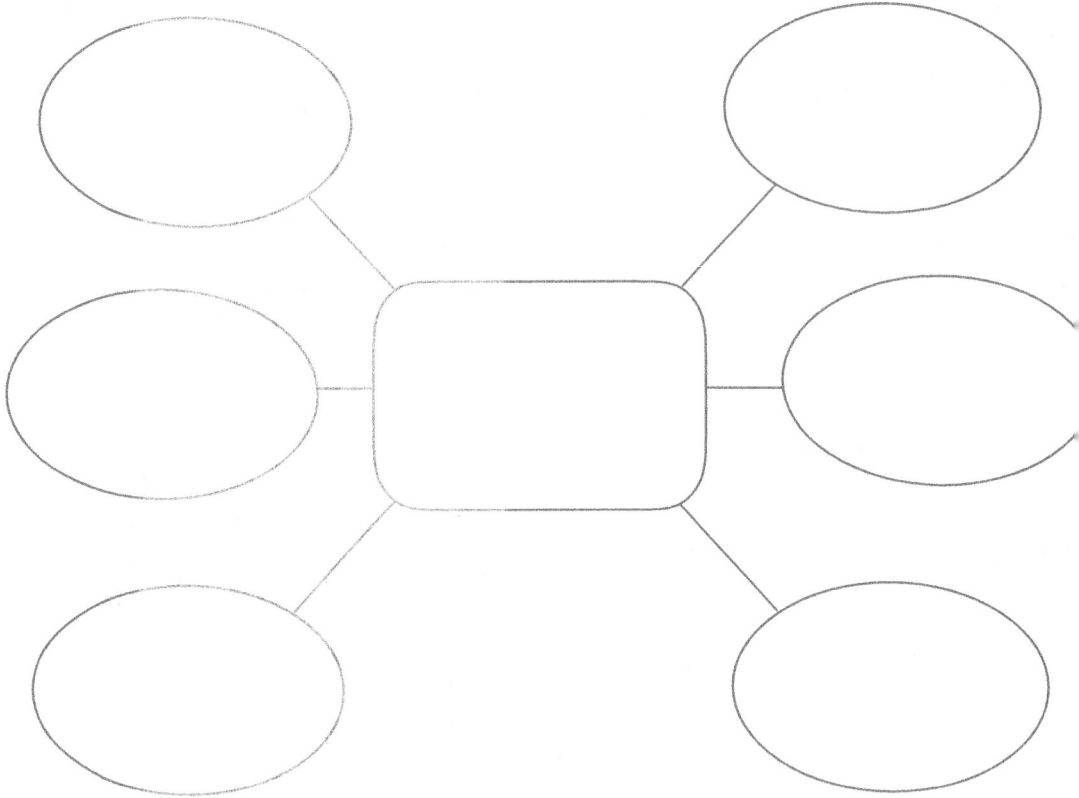

_____
_____
_____
_____
_____
_____
_____
_____

Did You like this book? Color the little sun, which most reflected your mood when reading this book

I like it !

I don't know

I don't like it

What this book is about

_____

_____

_____

_____

_____

_____

What is the main event of this book   What did You learn from this book

_____   _____

_____   _____

_____   _____

_____   _____

_____   _____

Book Review

Title

Author

Number of pages

Draw the main character

Book Review

Describe main character

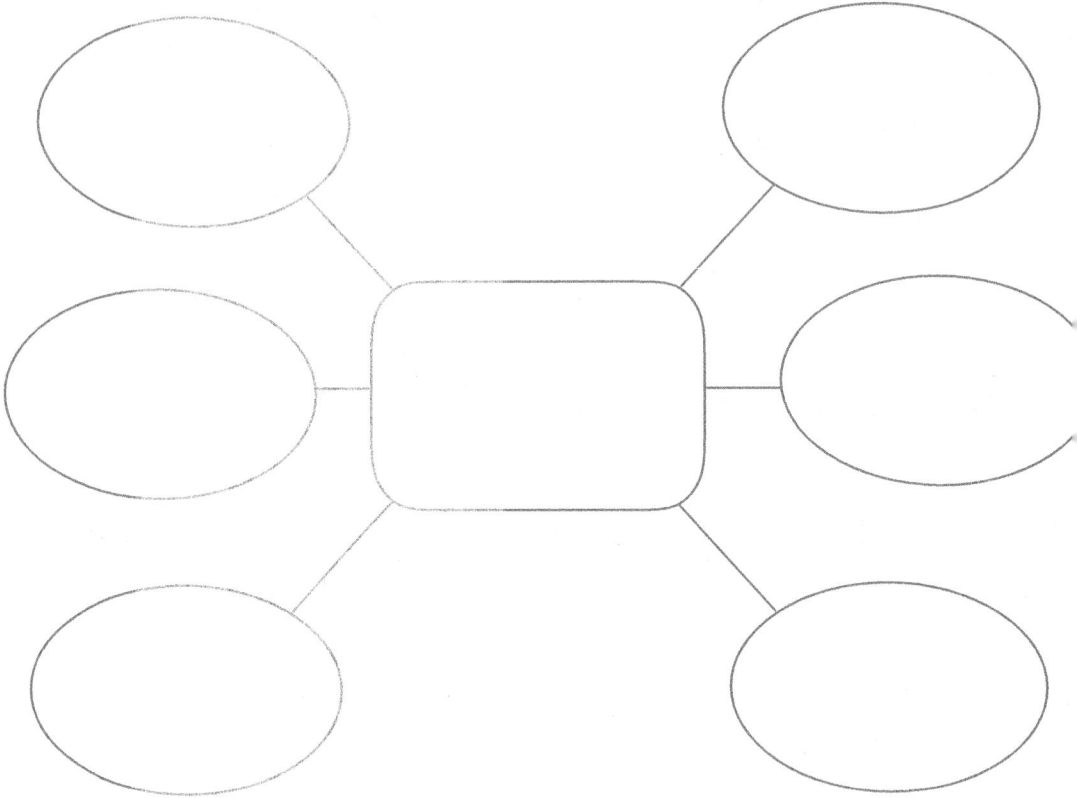

Did You like this book? Color the little sun, which most reflected your mood when reading this book

I like it !

I don't know

I don't like it

What this book is about

_____

_____

_____

_____

_____

_____

_____

What is the main event of this book   What did You learn from this book

_____   _____

_____   _____

_____   _____

_____   _____

_____   _____

Book Review

Title

Author

Number of pages

Draw the main character

Book Review

Describe main character

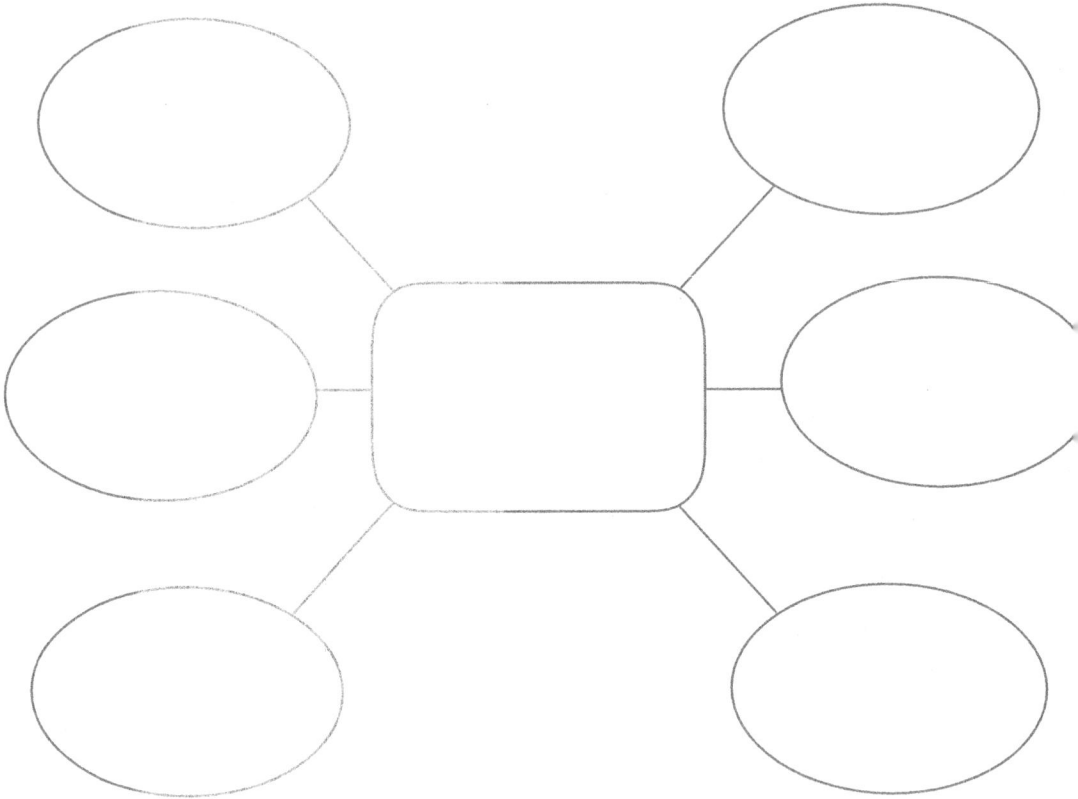

Did You like this book? Color the little sun, which most reflected your mood when reading this book

I like it !

I don't know

I don't like it

What this book is about

_____

_____

_____

_____

_____

_____

_____

What is the main event of this book   What did You learn from this book

_____   _____

_____   _____

_____   _____

_____   _____

_____   _____

_____   _____

Book Review

Title

Author

Number of pages

Draw the main character

Book Review

Describe main character

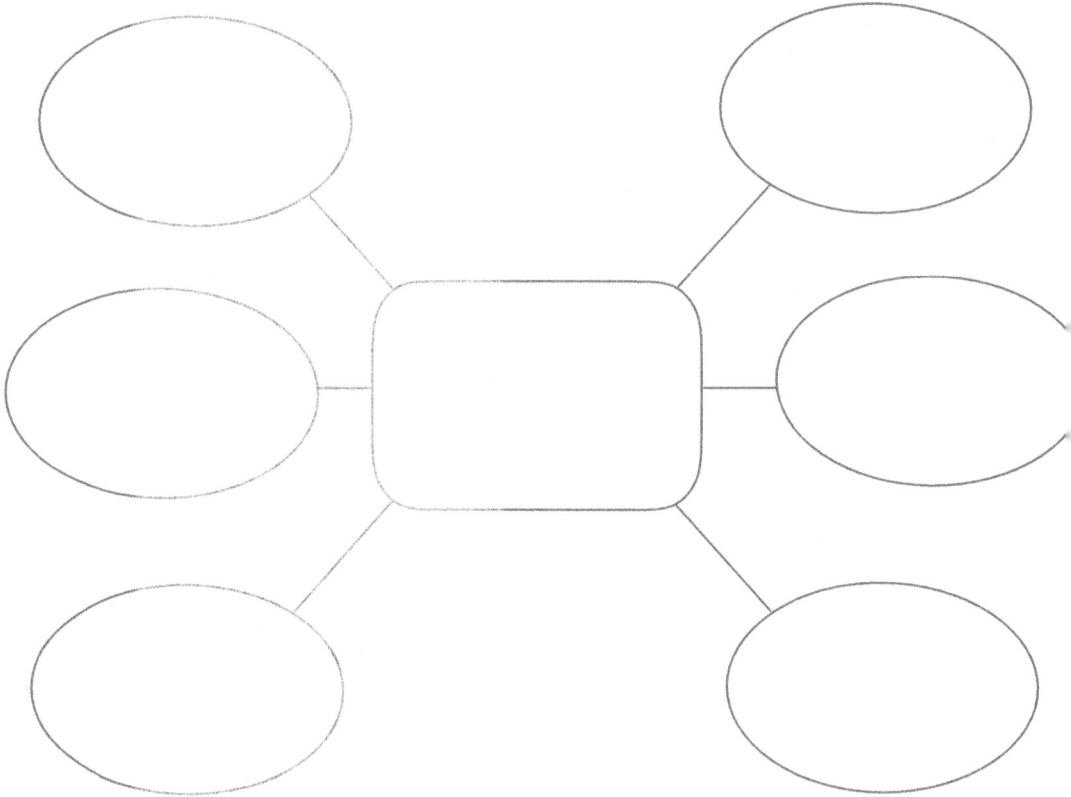

Did You like this book? Color the little sun, which most reflected your mood when reading this book

I like it !   I don't know   I don't like it

What this book is about

_____

_____

_____

_____

_____

_____

What is the main event of this book   What did You learn from this book

_____   _____

_____   _____

_____   _____

_____   _____

_____   _____

_____   _____

Book Review

Title

Author

Number of pages

Draw the main character

Book Review

Describe main character

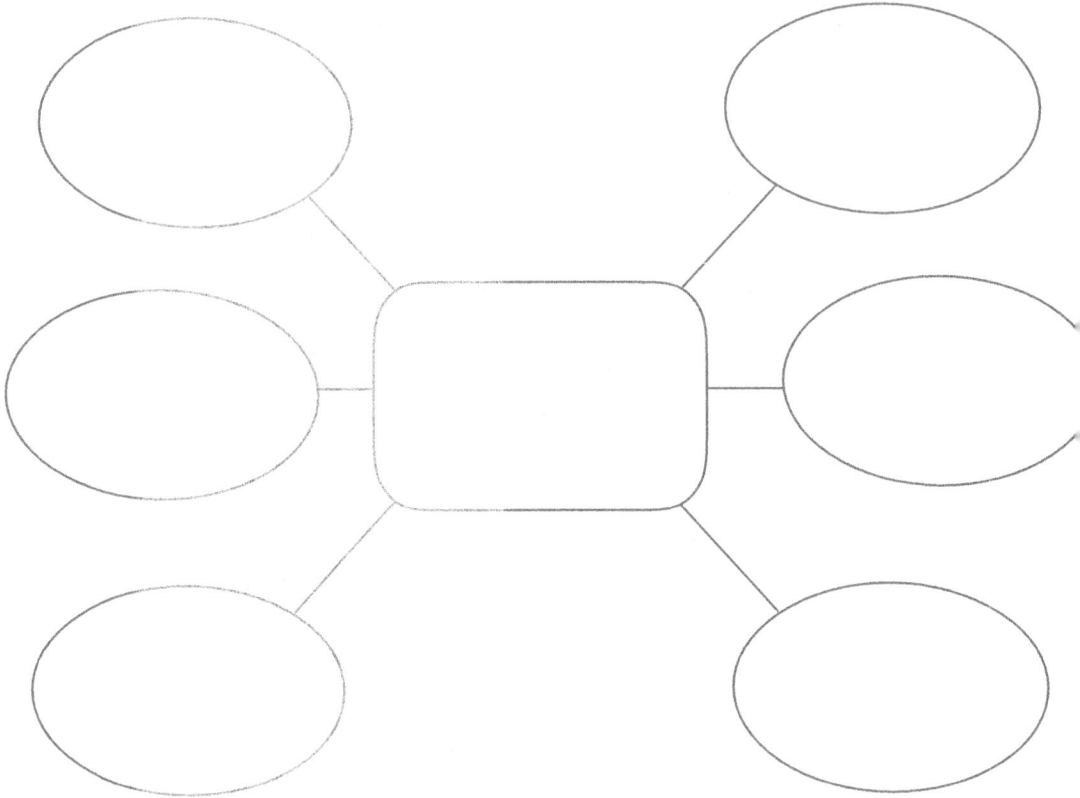

Did You like this book? Color the little sun, which most reflected your mood when reading this book

I like it !

I don't know

I don't like it

What this book is about

_____

_____

_____

_____

_____

_____

_____

What is the main event of this book   What did You learn from this book

Printed in Great Britain
by Amazon